Easy Logic
Tibetan Wisdom For Happiness and Success

Eric Brinkman

Standing on the Sky Press

Standing on the Sky Press

Published in the United States
Copyright © 2014 by Eric Brinkman

first edition

All rights reserved. No part of this publication may
be reproduced, stored in a retrieval system, or transmitted in any form or by any means without the
prior permission in writing of Standing in the Sky Press,
or as expressly permitted by law, or under
terms agreed with the appropriate reprographics rights
organization. Enquiries concerning reproduction
outside the scope of the above should be sent to
Standing in the Sky Press.

ISBN: 978-0-9914738-0-9

No responsibility for loss caused to any individual or organization acting on or refraining from action as a result
of the material in this publication can be accepted by the
publishers or author.

Editors: Amie Diller, Elly van der Pas
Proofreading: David Fishman
Page Layout: Katey Fetch
Cover: Rosa Van Grieken

*To all my teachers,
both seen and unseen*

Contents

Introduction	7
Chapter 1: Wisdom from the Roof of the World	10
Chapter 2: Hard Work & Money	14
Chapter 3: How to play the Game	18
Chapter 4: Making Money	26
Chapter 5: Better Health	33
Chapter 6: Relationships	37
Chapter 7: A Correct Syllogism	40
Chapter 8: The Key to It All	44
Chapter 9: Seeds Grow	51
Chapter 10: The True Cause of Health	55
Chapter 11: Negation	60
Chapter 12: Proof of Emptiness	67
Chapter 13: The True Cause of Relationships	75
Chapter 14: Another Proof for Emptiness	86
Chapter 15: The Emptiness of How Things Work	90
Chapter 16: Getting things to Work, Part Two	95
Chapter 17: The King of Reasons	98
Chapter 18: Following Up on a Syllogism	103
Chapter 19: Not Necessarily, My Friend	108
Chapter 20: Conclusion and Encouragement to Continue	111
Appendix A: The Three Tests	114
Appendix B: The Four Laws of Seeds	116
Appendix C: Debating	126
Appendix D: Sillygisms	130
Appendix E: Answer Key	134
Appendix F: Assumptions	167
Appendix G: Even Emptiness must be Empty	178
Appendix H: Additional Resources	180

Introduction

One day I was reading a book called "Mental Hacks" about how to improve your cognitive thinking, and I saw it had a chapter on logic. I love logic, so I flipped right to that chapter. Right away it had a great example to prove that human beings are not wired to think abstractly (most people cannot solve the problem with just pure numbers, but if they are told the numbers are drinking age limits they can solve it easily). This had a big impact on me, because as a logic teacher, I have always struggled with trying to understand why logic is so hard for my students to understand.

Years ago some students asked me to write a book, so I wrote my first logic workbook and cheerfully passed it out to them. No one used it. Then finally one student tried (thanks, Amie), and from listening to the questions she asked me, I quickly realized why no one was using it: it was too difficult, too abstract, and too much like trying to learn math.

Logic is very similar to math (well, in fact, you could say math is a subset of logic that only uses numbers). If you're like most people, you probably didn't like math, hated it in high school, and tried to avoid it as much as you could. Then you complained to all your friends that it was useless, and told them how you would never need or use it when you grew up.

Have you seen Peggie Sue Got Married, *where Peggie Sue goes back in time and tells her algebra teacher she knows, for a fact, she will never use algebra?*

But my experience of learning logic is very different. One of the classical reasons given in Tibetan monasteries for why you should study logic is so that you can know things that the eyes can't see. You can't see everything there is to know with your eyes. So, for me, learning logic was like being able to access a new world. Robert Thurman once used the word "psychonaut" to describe a Tibetan concept; I felt like that learning logic: through understanding how to think logically

For Example
Like subatomic particles, for example— the very building blocks of physical reality—which we can't see.

I became an astronaut or explorer of worlds unseen or unknowable by the human eye.

So my job, as I see it, is to show you how useful logic is, to show how useful it can be to know things that you otherwise couldn't know. Do you want to know how to be successful every time? Would you like all of your relationships to work out? How would you like to be sure that the plan you have to get healthy will work? Most of us are just guessing—but if you work out the logic, you can know what the results will be.

Hand in hand with that, I'm going to try to make reading this book as little like learning high school math as possible. To do this we'll use concrete examples, both so that you'll see the practical utility of learning to think logically, as well as be able to learn more quickly and easily (since our minds aren't wired to process abstract information).

So throughout this book we'll use lots of examples that apply directly to your life, so that you won't feel like Peggy Sue being forced back into taking high school math that you know you won't need.

But to begin, we'll start by asking, where do these ideas come from?

Chapter 1:
Wisdom from the Roof of the World

For centuries, unbeknownst to the rest of the world, Tibetans living on the "roof of the world" possessed a mental technology that allowed them to hone their thinking and produce some of the greatest minds the world has ever seen.

Unfortunately, this technology has not been readily available in the west. Cloaked in cultural differences and defended by a fierce language barrier, few people have even tried to discover its secrets.

When I was first exposed to Tibetan logic, I was told that it couldn't be translated into English and that you couldn't debate in English either. Neither of these beliefs is true— although, at the time, it was very difficult.

But from a Tibetan wisdom perspective, understanding logic is the key to reaching any goal. When we try to get things in our lives, most of us are just guessing if what we are doing will work or not. But with logic, you can work out with certainty what the

results of your actions will be, because cause and effect relationships are logical ones. Would you like to be healthy, find the partner of your dreams, reach success in life, and, in general, just be happy? Tibetan wisdom would say if you want to be sure to get these things, start by learning logic.

So my goal with this book is not only to bring this profound technology to you, in an easy to understand way, but to also to do it in such a way that you see its power to transform your life.

Gyeltsab Je Dharma Rinchen, one of the greatest Tibetan logicians of all time, said of his teacher, "The kindest thing he ever did for me was to teach me logic." Why? Because, according to the Tibetan wisdom tradition, there are two ways to know something: direct and indirect perception. Direct perception is easy; it's what you can feel, touch, taste, smell, and hear. How do you know the pen is blue? Because you're looking at a blue pen.

But there's another way to know things; we can call it indirect perception, deductive perception, reasoning, or simply logic.

Sometimes we also like to call indirect perception "clear thinking" to avoid the stigma of the word "logic." I once had someone come to a class I taught on "clear thinking" and admit to me that they would not have come if I had called the class "logic."

So my intent with this book is to teach how you can use this previously elusive technology to prove the truth of things for yourself. And we won't do it by talking about high falutin' philosophical concepts that would give you a headache trying to understand them; instead, we'll do it with things that matter to you: money, health, and relationships. How would you like to know if your business deal is going to make money? If this next job is the right one for you? If you should have the surgery or try homeopathic treatments? Which will work? What about the girl or guy you've been flirting with at work: should you ask them out?

Most of us are just guessing whether something will work out or not when we try things in our lives. But

Tibetan wisdom says you can know with certainty how these things are going to work out. Figure out logically what the result is going to be and then you don't have to worry. If done correctly, it must be the case that what you've worked out logically will come true.

So I'm going to try to break through the cultural barriers and language differences and teach Tibetan logic in a way that anyone can understand. So let's begin. I'll just start off by asking you a simple question: does hard work make money?

Chapter 2:
Hard Work & Money

When we were growing up, our mothers and fathers, school teachers, bosses, everyone told us that if you work hard good things will happen. The very successful American football coach Vince Lombardi said, "The dictionary is the only place that success comes before work. Work is the key to success, and hard work can help you accomplish anything."

We've been taught this or some variation of it all through our lives. Work hard and you will reach your goals, find a good job, and be successful. So we all know it's true, right? It's common sense.

In the Tibetan monasteries, when they're starting the thirteen year-old monks out on logic (one key to success: start them young!), they begin by teaching them a game. It's called "Three or Four Possibilities."

Between any two things (that share a relationship and which are not the same) either three or four of the following list of possibilities are true:

1. A but not B
2. B but not A
3. Both
4. Neither

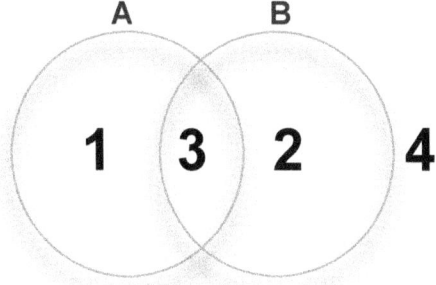

If you can find examples for all four possibilities then you have four possibilities, and if only three are possible then you have three possibilities.

 *Hint: If you find that only three possibilities are true, it will be because either #1 or #2 is not possible.*

Okay, so that was kind of abstract. Let's try to make it more concrete. Let's say that "A" is hard work and "B" is making money.

So, can you think of an example of someone who:

1. Works hard, but doesn't have money
2. Has money, but doesn't work hard
3. Works hard and has money
4. Doesn't work hard and doesn't have money

Can you? I can. Let's think of some examples. (1) For the first case, I usually think, "me." Just kidding. But I think all of us can think of someone who works hard yet still is always broke. I have this mental picture in my mind of a photo I once saw of an Indian woman during a heat wave breaking rocks on the side of the road. I was told those women barely make enough money at the end of the day to buy plain rice to eat. (2) A trust fund baby, someone who inherited the money, or someone who hit the lottery. (3) Warren Buffet or any successful workaholic. (4) For this one I usually say, "My cousin." Everyone has one of these guys in their family; always bumming money because they can't hold down a job.

So for "hard work" and "money" all four possibilities exist.

So who cares? What does playing that game teach? Well, a couple of things, but for our purposes right now, the important thing we can know here is that the relationship between hard work and money is **not** a cause and effect relationship.

If someone can work hard and not make money (like a volunteer, for example) or have lots of money and not be working hard, then there's no necessary relationship between working hard and making money. That is, it's not a cause and effect relationship. There may be some correlation, but hard work is not the cause of having or making money.

In other words, everyone who ever told us if you work hard you will necessarily make money was wrong.

Exercises

1. Think of some of the positive reasons for studying logic; go from general to specific (that is, starting with "It will improve my mind" or "It will help me think more clearly and solve problems better" down to "I'll be able to figure out how to solve that problem at work more efficiently").

2. Play the three or four possibilities game. Start with something simple, like "red" and "ball." Then try something more complex, such as "intelligent" and "rich" or "beautiful" and "has a great relationship."

Chapter 3:
How to play the Game

Now that you're familiar with the three or four possibilities game, we'll get down to studying more formal logic: official Tibetan logic all centers on the use of *syllogisms*. So what's a syllogism?

Unfortunately, this part is going to be a little bit difficult. But hang in there; it's worth it. (Eventually, I'll prove it to you.)

But let's start off by saying it doesn't have to be so hard, and you might already be a little bit familiar with them. **Aristotelian** logic uses syllogisms, and they are very similar to Tibetan syllogisms.

In fact, we think there might be a connection. When Alexander the Great invaded India, he himself was a student of Aristotle and brought along a student of Aristotle to debate. After he

conquered a city, in his own enlightened way, he asked, "Show me your philosophers." They would trot them out, and this student of Aristotle and the local philosophers would have a go.

Alexander then left, but before he left he would choose and leave behind a Greek general to run things. The descendants of these Aristotle-trained generals, in many cases, eventually became the local king. The first sutra that has debating in it in the Tibetan wisdom tradition is called "The Questions of King Milinda." In this sutra, a Buddhist monk debates with a King using syllogisms, and this king would have been the descendant of one of the Greek generals Alexander left behind. This is the first formal debate text we have. Coincidence? So it's possible that Aristotle students had an influence on the evolution of the Tibetan wisdom debate tradition.

For example, maybe you've seen or heard this before:

> **John is a doctor.**
> **All doctors are humans.**
> **Therefore, John is human.**

This is **Aristotelian** logic. Not so hard. So Tibetan logic is just a variation on this. So let's

ⓘ *More Info Please: For more on the differences between Aristotelian and Tibetan logic, see Appendix F, "Assumptions."*

start. All Tibetan syllogisms have three parts: a subject, an assertion, and a reason.

Actually, Tibetan syllogisms can also have a fourth part—an example—but we'll talk about this more later.

Simply:

1) Subject - what you're talking about
2) Assertion - what you are trying to prove
3) Reason - why you think your assertion is true

Not so hard, right? Okay, so let's try one:

<u>Syllogism #1</u>
(1) Consider a Ford Mustang,
(2) It's a car,
(3) Because I like monkeys.

Okay, so here we have the first syllogism we'll work with. It has the three necessary parts: (1) a subject (a Ford Mustang), (2) what we're trying to prove (it's a car), and (3) a reason (because I like monkeys). So we're good, right?

Of course not. And now you're thinking, "This is why I never bothered to learn the rules of logic. It's just a mind game; there's no point." Well, hold on a minute.

In Tibetan logic, the definition of a reason is "that which is given as a reason." So anything given as a reason is a reason. But that doesn't make it a correct reason.

So here's the point of all debate: how do we determine if a reason is correct or not? According to the Tibetans, a correct reason is defined as, "That which passes the three tests." Okay, so what are the three tests?

Here's where you might have to take notes. If you bought this as a book, maybe fold down the corner of this page. Or if you have an electronic version, go ahead and bookmark this one, because you have to know these.

> **More Info:**
> *If you forget the three tests you can also refer to Appendix A: "The Three Tests," on page 114.*

In fact, learning how to use these three tests is the key to understanding how to practice logical thinking. This is it—this what you have to learn to be able to make better decisions in your life to help yourself and others.

Test #1: Is there a relationship between the subject and the reason? That is, does the reason apply to the subject?

So here we just have to ask ourselves, is there a connection or a relationship between the (1) subject and the

(3) reason? In this example, is there some relationship between Ford Mustangs and monkeys?

Not that I'm aware of. So this syllogism fails the first test, which means this syllogism is not correct. In other words, it's not true, or you could say it's false.

So lets try again. Consider the following syllogism:

Syllogism #2
(1) Consider a Ford Mustang,
(2) It is a car,
(3) Because it exists.

Is this one true or false? There's no way to know without running the three tests. So what's test #1? Does the (3) reason apply to the (1) subject?

Test #1: Does the reason, (3) something that exists, apply to the subject, (1) a Ford Mustang?

Yes. Ford Mustangs exist, so as long as the one you are talking about isn't one that doesn't, this syllogism passes the first test.

But does passing the first test mean this syllogism is true? No. Unfortunately, there are still two more tests. So let's learn the second test.

*At this point I should mention—and this is very important—a thing that does not exist **cannot** share a relationship with anything. For example, how long are the horns on the head of a rabbit? You can't describe something that doesn't exist; it can't have qualities. And since it can't have qualities, it can't share a relationship with anything else—that is, something that does not exist will always fail test #1.*

Test #2: If the (3) reason is true, then the (2) assertion **must** always be true.

So in this example, how would we apply the second test? Something like this: if something exists, must it be a car?

So... no, that's not right. This test is called **positive necessity.** The thing here that is important to catch is the word "must." If the reason is true, the assertion must be true. So is it true that if something exists it must be a car? No, of course not. So this syllogism fails the second test, and so it is therefore, again, not true—we can say it's false.

We'll give many more examples to make sure you understand this concept, but one more thing to point out here is that the order is very important.

To check for positive necessity, you should check "if 3, then 2," **not** "if 2, then 3." Don't get it backwards! In other words, the test is: if something exists, must it be a car? Not: if it's a car, it must exist (which would be true).

So again, in this example just because something exists doesn't mean it has to be a car. Therefore this syllogism is also false.

Exercises

Consider the following syllogism and answer the questions about it:

<u>Syllogism #3</u>
**(1) Consider John,
(2) He is a human being,
(3) Because he's a doctor.**

1. What is the subject of this syllogism?

2. What is the assertion (the thing it's trying to prove)?

3. What is the reason does it use?

4. What is the first test in this case? (Use this example in your answer.)

5. What is the second test? (Use this example in your answer.)

Chapter 4: Making Money

So let's use a more serious example. We played the three or four possibilities game in chapter one to show that hard work is not the cause of making money (because there's no necessary relationship between them). Let's try to write out what we learned before as a more formal syllogism and evaluate whether what we discovered is actually true or false:

<u>Syllogism #4</u>
(1) Consider money,
(2) I'm going to get some,
(3) Because I work hard.

This is what we did in chapter one, expressed as a syllogism. So we already know it's false, but let's run the tests now to make sure.

Test #1: Is there a relationship between (1) money and (3) hard work?

What do you think? We know ultimately that there isn't. But do you know someone who works hard and makes money? If so, then this one is okay. So what do we do next? Does that mean this reason is good? Not necessarily, we have to run the second test.

Test #2: If someone (3) works hard, is it the case that they *must* (2) get some money?

I quit my job at Cornell University to do some volunteer work at a Buddhist university in Arizona. In the desert. In the summertime. And I can tell you how much I got paid.

Nada.

So I know for myself, this one is false.

But we already knew that this one was false, so let's try another one:

<u>Syllogism #5</u>
(1) Consider real estate,
(2) I should invest in it,
(3) Because it always gets a good return.

Is this true? I think many people have said this, from experts in economics to most real estate investors.

But Tibetan logic says the only way to know if this "sure thing" is true is to check to see if it passes the three tests. So let's check.

Test #1: Is there a relationship between the (1) subject and the (3) reason? That is, is there a connection between real estate and always getting a return?

The thing to key on here in this example is the word "always." Like we said in the last chapter, for something to share a relationship with something else, both of those things must exist. So let's consider the reason "real estate deals always get a return." Is that reason something that exists or not; that is, is that statement true? Of course not; many real estate deals have ended with someone losing their shirt (there are no "sure things" in life except death and taxes). So, since a real estate investment that *always* gets a return doesn't exist, that means that real estate doesn't share a relationship with, or you could say that it doesn't have anything in common with, something that doesn't exist, which in this case is the proposition that real estate always gets a good return.

 *Or, another way to think about it is to think that something true cannot share a relationship with something false. So, if the subject doesn't exist or the reason is false, then there cannot be a relationship between the subject and the reason. For example, consider the subject "horns on a rabbit." Rabbits do not have horns, so the subject "rabbits with horns" does not exist—which means it cannot share a relationship with the reason. Conversely, consider the reason "because the sun is green." That reason is false, because a green sun does not exist. So similarly, it cannot share a relationship with a subject.*

Therefore, since something that doesn't exist can't share a relationship with something else, this syllogism fails the first test.

For Example
We said that things that do not exist cannot share a relationship with something else. For example, do monkeys and three-headed pink elephants have the same eye color? How long are the horns on a rabbit? What color is a rainbow under the sea? Those questions don't make any sense, because a thing that does not exist cannot have qualities or share a relationship with something else.

And again, we prove that another common sense argument is not true.

But okay, everyone knows real estate doesn't *always* get a good return. That doesn't mean I shouldn't invest in it. Does it?

Let's try another one:

Syllogism #6
(1) Consider real estate,
(2) I should invest in it,
(3) Because sometimes it gets a good return.

So, what about this one; is it true?

Well, we have to run the tests. So what's test number one?

Test #1: Is there a relationship between the (1) subject and the (3) reason? Meaning here, does real estate sometimes get a return?

I think we can say yes here, so there is a connection. (I don't really know anyone myself who made a lot of money through real estate, but I googled it and evidently a lot of people have, including Thomas Jefferson, who bought Louisiana from the French.)

But before we can say this syllogism is true, we also have to run test #2. Do you remember it? (If not, review page 23.)

Test #2: If the (3) reason is true, then the (2) assertion must be true.

So here what that would mean is if something gets a good return sometimes, you necessarily should invest in it. Is that true? If something sometimes works, should you always use it? That doesn't really make sense, does it? Wouldn't it be the case that, if you always used something, you would want it to always work, not just work sometimes?

So I would say it fails this test.

So now, since you know how to use the first two tests to check if a syllogism is true, I've included some exercises on the next page that you can do to hone your knowledge.

Exercises

Consider the following syllogism and then try to answer the questions about it:

<u>Syllogism #7</u>
(1) Consider the stock market,
(2) I should invest in it,
(3) Because it's my best chance to get a good return.

1. What is the subject?

2. What is the assertion (the thing it's trying to prove)?

3. What is the reason?

4. What is the first test in this case? (Use this example in your answer.)

5. What is the second test? (Use this example in your answer.)

6. Is this syllogism true or false? (Does it pass both tests?)

Chapter 5:
Better Health

We've been talking about money a lot for these examples so far, so let's discuss another area where we can use logic: to fix our health. So many options, so many decisions. What should I do? Jog? Is eating less red meat better for me? Is wine good for my heart?

We're all asking ourselves these questions. The problem is we don't have a tool to evaluate all of the many different options that we're being given. So let's try using our new tool for evaluating the veracity of some claims made by health gurus and the media.

<u>Syllogism #8</u>
(1) Consider my health,
(2) It will improve,
(3) Because I practice yoga to improve my health.

I can do this one because I teach yoga, and I received so many benefits from practicing it myself. But is this syllogism true? Sounds good, maybe it is. But the only way to be sure is to run our three tests.

Test #1: Is there a relationship between the (1) subject and the (3) reason? Yes, the reason makes it explicit—"I practice yoga to improve my health."

Test #2: If the (3) reason is true, then the (2) assertion *must* always be true. Is this the case? In other words, if I practice yoga, will my health necessarily improve?

I have a joke I like to tell to illustrate this. Three people walk into a yoga class...

As each of them walk out of class I ask them, "What did you think of the class?"

The first person, let's call her Mary, says, "Wow, that was so great! I feel so wonderful! When can we do it again?"

The second person comes out; let's call him Brian (okay, this part really happened). The same question: "How did you like the class?"

"Oh, it was okay. I think I prefer jogging though."

The third person comes out. "What did you think of the class?"

In response all I get is a straggled cry. "Oh god, my neck. Where's a chiropractor!"

So I'm making a joke, but the point of it is true: yoga won't necessarily make you healthy, and lots of people get hurt doing yoga every day.

> ⓘ *In fact, the* **New York Times** *reported back in 2007 that the number of yoga injuries treated in emergency rooms or doctors' offices had risen to 5,500 cases in the U.S. alone.*

Some people like it, some people don't, some people will see their health improve, and other people will get injured.

So what is the answer to our syllogism?

Not necessarily. Just because you practice yoga doesn't mean your health will improve.

 **Exercises**

Consider the following syllogism and then try to answer the questions about it:

<u>Syllogism #9</u>
(1) Consider chemotherapy,
(2) It will remove my cancer,
(3) Because my doctor says it is my best option.

1. What is the subject?

2. What is the assertion?

3. What is the reason?

4. What is the first test in this case? (Use this example in your answer.)

5. What is the second test? (Use this example in your answer.)

Chapter 6: Relationships

So we've discussed money and health. What else could Tibetan logic help us to think more clearly about?

<u>Syllogism #10</u>
(1) Consider the girl/guy of my dreams,
(2) I will meet her/him,
(3) Because I'm using an executive dating service.

True or false? Again, I'm being slightly humorous here, but the truth is we think this way. Or substitute in your preferred method: online dating, hitting the bars, or asking friends and relatives to set you up. Whatever your preferred method is, will it work? That is, it is true?

How can we know? You have to run the three tests.

Test #1: Is there a connection between the (1) subject and the (3) reason? Sure, executive dating services are trying to match up men and women. So as long as you did actually hire a dating service, this syllogism passes the first test. (If you hadn't actually hired a dating service, then this would fail the first test, because a dating service you hired when you didn't hire one doesn't exist. And as we said before, a thing that doesn't exist can't share a relationship with anything else.)

Test #2: If the (3) reason is true, then the (2) assertion *must* always be true. So, if someone hires an executive dating service, do they always meet the man or women of their dreams?

Of course not. If they did, then everyone would use one. One of my teachers likes to use an aspirin to get this point across. Consider the following:

Syllogism #11
(1) Consider my headache,
(2) It will go away,
(3) Because I took an aspirin.

True or false? Well, if it's true then it should pass the second test: if you (3) take an aspirin, does your (2) headache always go away. If not, then you have to agree that the aspirin is not the cause of removing your headache. If it were, then it should work every time—

because a cause isn't a cause unless it produces a result (and conversely, placebos wouldn't seem to work either, but that's another subject).

Exercises

Consider this syllogism, and then answer the following questions.

<u>Syllogism #12</u>
(1) Consider red lipstick,
(2) It will make me more attractive,
(3) Because the man I'm interested in will think it's sexy.

1. What is the subject?

2. What is the assertion?

3. What is the reason?

4. What is the first test in this case? (Use this example in your answer.)

5. What is the second test? (Use this example in your answer.)

6. Is this syllogism true or false?

Chapter 7: A Correct Syllogism

Now that we have some idea of what an incorrect syllogism looks like, let's take a look at one that's true. Consider the following:

<u>Syllogism #13</u>
(1) Consider a sound,
(2) It's not the color red,
(3) Because it doesn't have color.

So is this one true or false? The only way to know is to run the tests:

Test #1: Is it true that sound does not have a color?

So since there is no relationship between sound and color—that is, sound does not have color—this syllogism passes the first test.

Test #2: If something does not have color, is it true that it must not be red?

This one is also correct. The easiest way to check for positive necessity is to do one simple test. If I took away all of one thing, would that take away all of the other? So, for example, if I take away all colors (blue, green, orange, fuchsia) would that also take away the color red? Yes, because red is a color.

Since this is our first syllogism to pass the first two tests, now you get to learn the third, final test. This one is simple; it's just a variation on the previous test. The last test was called "positive necessity," so this one is called "negative necessity." What that means is, if the (2) assertion is negated, would it also negate the (3) reason?

Wow, that's abstract. So again, let's make it concrete. If something is red (that is, not not red), is it also true that it is (not not) a color? Don't get confused by the negation; that is, all the "nots." Not + not = positive. (Ugh! Math!)

> ⓘ *For a detailed discussion of negation, see* **Chapter Ten: Negation.**

Yes, if something is red, then it has to be a color. There's a lot of negation in that last example; I'm sorry! Later we'll work on understanding negation in more detail.

For now, just write down or take notes on what the third test is—keeping in mind that the order is important, just like it is with positive necessity: the test is if not 2, not 3. If you check if not 3 not 2, you're doing the test backward.

If you don't understand everything yet, don't worry! We'll practice running the three tests with lots of examples, and in the next chapter you're going to learn the secret to answering almost any logical puzzle.

> *For Example*
> In Syllogism #2, the third test would be: if something is not a car, does it not exist? The third test is not: if something does not exist, is it not a car? Don't get it backwards! It's not true that if something is not a car, it does not exist (you are not a car, but you exist), so that syllogism is false.

Exercises

Read the following syllogism and answer the questions:

<u>Syllogism #14</u>
(1) Consider a car,
(2) It's not a motorcycle,
(3) Because cars and motorcycles are not the same.

1. Please write down the subject, assertion, and reason for this assertion.

2. Write out the first test for this syllogism.

3. Write out the second test.

4. Write out the third test.

5. Is this syllogism true of false?

6. Try to write out a correct syllogism on your own, run the tests to make sure!

Chapter 8:
The Key to It All

So back in chapter three we talked about how to make money. We showed that some "common sense" ideas, like hard work or real estate investing, are false, (that is, they are not the real cause of money). So now that we know all the tests for determining what is true, what is the right answer?

Here's the big secret. Many philosophies (such as existentialism or subjectivism) fail in the end because they fail to understand one key concept that is at the core of the Tibetan system. It's called emptiness.

There's a lot of misunderstanding about what this idea really means. Schopenhauer, for example, classically misunderstood it and used it to come up with nihilism. But emptiness doesn't mean nothing exists or nothing matters (in fact, it means the opposite, but we'll get to that).

What emptiness means simply is that nothing has any meaning by itself. The example we often use to illustrate this is a pen. If I show you a pen, what makes it a pen? Where does a "pen" come from?

Because the fact is that the rods and cones of the eye can't see a pen. Our eyes can only see shape and color. The eye sees black and long, thin, round cylinder. So where does "pen" come from?

Tibetan logic says it has to be coming from us, because it can't be coming from the object; that is, that the object is empty of being a pen by itself. How do we know this? Because if you hold up a black, long, thin cylinder to a dog, he doesn't see a pen. What does he see? Maybe something to chew on or something he wants to bury in the backyard.

Why? You might think, "Because dogs are stupid." But if you think that, you missed the point. If it's because of the dog that he doesn't see a pen, then it's because of us that we do. If the pen were somehow *in* the pen, then the dog, even if he were stupid, would have to see a pen. If I see a pen and the dog sees a chew toy, is the object somehow different? That is, did the object somehow change? Am I seeing a different object?

If it's not different, then the reason we see something different has to be because it's coming from us. We're applying the idea "pen" to the long, thin, black stick. In Tibetan logic, this is called dependent origination, which is a fancy way of saying, "Where do things come from?"

If the object is empty of being a pen—if it doesn't have any magical "penness" inside it somehow (if it did the dog would have to see it as a pen also)—then where does pen come from?

Dependent origination says it comes from a seed in our mind. You see black, long, thin cylinder and a seed ripens in your mind that says, "That's a pen." The dog has a different seed in his mind ("That's a chew toy"), so he sees something different. And you have to say that is true, because for a dog, it's not a pen (unless you've ever seen a dog write with a pen?).

So where do these mental seeds come from? The Tibetan wisdom tradition says from how you treat other people. Your mind is like a video camera; it records everything you do, say, or think. This gets recorded as a mental seed, and then when that seed ripens it plays it back to you.

So consider the following syllogism:

Syllogism #15
(1) Consider money,
(2) I'm going to get some,
(3) Because I give money away.

True or false? The only way to know is to run the tests. So let's try it.

Test #1: Is there a relationship between (1) money and (3) giving money away?

Yes, in this case simply because in both statements we're discussing money. You can't give away money without there being money. So here (1) the subject, money, does apply to (3) the reason (giving money away).

Test #2: If I give away money, must I get some?

For this one, I have to explain some more things about mental seeds. In the Tibetan wisdom tradition, there are four rules that apply to seeds and how they work; they're called the "Four Laws of Seeds." The first of these rules says, "Seeds are definite." What this means is that if you do something—which plants a seed in your mind—the result you get must be similar. Just like physical seeds, if you plant a watermelon you're not going to get an eggplant.

>  *This concept is not unique the Tibetan tradition. Jesus also said, no "Grapes of thorns, or figs of thistles." Meaning, you can't get a grape by planting a thorn bush or a fig from a thistle; that is, results must resemble their causes.*

In the same way, if you give something then you must get something. This is cause and effect.

But wait a minute! That sounds great (I've heard it before), but it's not true. I've given things away before and never received anything in return.

We'll talk about it.

I'll prove all this to you later, but for now, assuming that the first law of seeds is true, does our syllogism past the second test? That is, if you (3) give money away (which plants a seed) must you (2) get money in the future? Yes, the first law of seeds says you must.

So if you want to make money, according to Tibetan philosophy, the only way to be sure is to plant the seeds for it by giving away money first.

Exercises

1. Write out the third test for syllogism #15.

Consider the following syllogism and answer the questions about it:

<u>Syllogism #16</u>
(1) Consider my real estate investments,
(2) They will get a good return,
(3) Because I created the cause (by planting a mental seed through being generous).

2. Write out the subject, assertion, and reason.

3. Write out the first test.

4. Write out the second test.

5. Write out the third test.

Consider the following syllogism and answer the questions about it:

<u>Syllogism #17</u>
(1) Consider money,
(2) I'm not going to have enough,
(3) Because I don't give it away.

6. Write out the subject, assertion, and reason.

7. Write out the first test.

8. Write out the second test.

9. Write out the third test.

Chapter 9:
Seeds Grow

But wait a second! If I have to give money before I can make money, how am I ever going to get ahead? I've seen people who give away all their money; all they end up being is broke.

Well, again, to understand here how mental seeds work you just have to look at how physical seeds work. I love fresh juice; let's say I just finished my glass of fresh-squeezed orange juice, but I'd like some more. What do I do? Let's say I pull out a seed from my orange pulp and plant it in the backyard. Then I get more oranges, right?

Of course not. At least not right away. It takes about four to six years for an orange tree to grow and really start producing oranges. In a nutshell, this is why we can't understand cause and effect: we're always trying to find cause and effect in the moment, when there is none.

Say for example I say something nice to my partner and then, in return, she yells at me. I think, "Wow, I'm not saying anything nice to her again. She's a jerk." Remember, the first law of karma says the cause must resemble the result. So in this example, why doesn't it look that way? The reason why they don't match up is because *there is no cause and effect in the moment*. Saying something nice to my partner and immediately expecting them to say something nice back is exactly like putting an orange seed in my backyard and immediately expecting more oranges.

In Tibetan philosophy we call this the *time gap*. Again, in a nutshell, it's why we can't really make any sense out of cause and effect: sometimes we yell at someone, and we get what we want; sometimes we yell at someone, and we don't get what we want; sometimes we don't yell at someone, and we get what we want; and sometimes we don't yell at someone, and we don't get what we want. Why? Because there's no cause and effect there—we're always looking for a connection in the moment for why things happen, but the truth is that the cause for what's happening now was planted a long time ago.

Similarly, just like the fact that physical seeds take time to grow is the fact that when a mental seed grows the result it produces can be much greater. A one ounce orange seed can produce a thousand pound tree that produces thousands of oranges—an average tree produces three to five hundred oranges per season for up to 100 years. Mental seeds are the same, and this is in fact the second law of mental seeds: seeds are increasing.

So, why should you give money to get money? Done properly, a small act of giving can produce a much larger result. Maybe you don't really care about money (after all, it isn't the real cause for happiness), but if what we're saying about mental seeds is true, one small act of generosity could plant a seed that could make you wealthy for life. Wouldn't that be nice?

Exercises

1. Write out the first law of seeds.

2. Write out the second law of seeds.

Consider the following syllogism, and then answer the subsequent questions:

<u>Syllogism #18</u>
(1) Consider giving ten dollars,
(2) The result I get will be much larger (I will get more than ten dollars in the future),
(3) Because mental seeds grow.

3. Please write out the subject, assertion, and reason.

4. Then write out the three tests. Is this syllogism true or false?

Chapter 10:
The True Cause of Health

So going back to our discussion about health, how do we improve our health? Is it jogging or less red meat? Knowing what we know now, consider the following syllogism:

<u>Syllogism #19</u>
(1) Consider my health,
(2) It will improve,
(3) Because I practice yoga.

True or false? This one passes the first test, because both the subject and the reason have to do with me (*my* health and *my* yoga practice).

Just because you practice yoga doesn't mean your health will improve; you could get injured. If this doesn't sound familiar then go back and review chapter 4.

But we did this one already—it's false because it fails the second test.

So how do we fix it?

Syllogism #20
(1) Consider my yoga practice,
(2) It will improve my health,
(3) Because I take care of sick people.

True or not true? The only way to know for sure it to run the tests.

Test #1: Is there a relationship between the (1) subject (your yoga practice, jogging, etc.) and the (3) reason (because I take care of sick people)?

The simple answer here is "yes," because I am referring to myself in both the subject (my practice) and the reason (I take care of sick people). Remember, test #1 is just asking if there is a connection between the subject and the reason. So the subject relates to me (we're talking about *my* practice) and the reason relates to me (*I* take care of sick people) so there is a relationship between the subject and the reason. So, if there is a relationship, then we need to run the second test.

> *If you don't agree with any of this, we'll discuss how to argue the point logically in chapter seventeen, "Following Up on a Syllogism."*

Test #2: If I take care of sick people, must my health improve?

Tibetan philosophy would say yes, because this is the very cause (the seed you need to plant) for health. In other words, if I take care of someone who is sick, that plants a seed for health. And must that be true? Yes, because the fourth law of seeds says that if you plant a seed you must get a result.

And now you know all four laws of seeds. Again, if you need to review please see Appendix B, "The Four Laws of Seeds."

And just for the sake of completion, since now we know what the third test is we should run that one too.

Test #3: If the (2) assertion is not true, the (3) reason must also be false.

So here in this example, test #3 would mean that if you do not help sick people your health will not improve. Is that true? Well, one answer would be to just reverse the logic above, but that also just happens to be the third law of seeds: if you don't create the cause, you can't get the result.

Again, this is almost true by definition: how could something be a result if it didn't have a cause? That wouldn't make any sense. So everything that is a result must have a cause, and the third law of seeds says explicitly that without that cause, no result is possible.

To use our previous metaphor, would you expect watermelon to grow in your backyard if you never planted seeds for it in your garden? Would you just stand at the window hoping, "Watermelon, watermelon, watermelon…"? That would be crazy. So the third law of seeds says that explicitly: don't expect a result if you didn't plant the cause for what you want.

So here in this case, if you want to be healthy, you have to plant the seed for that, by helping someone else with their health.

Exercises

Consider the next syllogism and answer the questions that follow:

<u>Syllogism #21</u>
(1) Consider eating healthy,
(2) It will improve my health,
(3) Because I'm already overweight.

1. Write out the subject, assertion, and reason.

2. Run the three tests; is this syllogism true or false?

3. If it's false, correct it so that it becomes true.

Chapter 11: Negation

So why do we run the third test? You may have noticed from our previous syllogisms (the last one, for example) that it seems that if a syllogism that fails the second test it will also fail the third test. If that's so, why bother to run the third test?

One reason is that it teaches us to think in terms of negation. There are two reasons why this is important: one is that you need to be able to not be confused when debating if negation comes up (did you follow that one?). Again, the simple rule they teach in the monastery is just add them up: if there are an odd number of negatives your statement is negative, and if you get an even number your statement is positive. (Math, I know).

So let's practice: The pen is not not not black.

Is the pen black? Three "nots" is odd, so the pen is not black.

Let's try another one: nothing is not anything other than that which is coming from your seeds.

Positive or negative?

This is the other reason for learning to understand negation. The definition in the Tibetan wisdom tradition for dependent origination is, "A projection on parts forced on us by seeds." Leaving the parts bit out for now, our minds see the idea of a thing ("pen") based on the seeds we have planted in the past.

So what's the definition of our one key, that essential idea that explains the nature of all things? There are several we can use, but one is, "Nothing is other than a projection on parts forced on us by our seeds."

All things have parts. For example, when you look at a pen we're talking about its shape and color: the black and long, thin shape that the eye sees. When we talk about mental things they have duration: the moments that make up a thought, for example. Every thought must have a beginning, middle, and end.

Did you catch it? What we did was add negation ("nothing") to our definition of dependent origination. There are two really important things to realize about this: one is the relationship between dependent origination and emptiness. Tibetan philosophy says they are two sides of the same coin; to talk about one is to talk about the other.

> ⓘ *To learn more about dependent origination and how you can use it to prove emptiness, read Chapter 17, "The King of Reasons."*

The other important thing to realize is that emptiness must involve negation. If someone tries to explain emptiness to you and uses positive language to describe it, you automatically know that they don't know what they're talking about (or they do, but what they're talking about isn't emptiness), *because emptiness, by its very definition, is always negating something*.

Why this is important is because in the Tibetan wisdom tradition not understanding emptiness—the true nature of all things—is the source of all our pain. We don't have the time here in this book to discuss it deeply, but they say, based on our misunderstanding of how things really work—what the real causes of things are—we all have a mistaken sense of reality. Then based on this mistaken sense of reality, we all make mistakes. And these mistakes we make, based on our misunderstanding, must inevitably lead us to pain.

For example, your boss (or your partner or your parents or your child) yells at you. You mistake their real nature; that is, you forget that they are empty—you're just seeing shapes and colors—and you think they are bad from their own side, which has nothing to do with your seeds or how your seeds are forcing you to see them. Then based on that, you yell back at them. But this only plants another seed to see someone else yell at you. And then you yell back at them again, thus continuing the same loop of behaviors and experiences. We call this a downward spiral.

So this is what emptiness negates: the person yelling at you, independent of how you have treated others in the past. They are not out there, independent of you, or separate from you and how you have treated others in the same way in the past. The eye only sees red, round shape and the ears only hear decibels. Your mind sees those parts, and then projects on to them the perception of them that you are seeing. If you stopped yelling at people your mind would see the same shapes and colors (and decibels) and force you to see something else: excited joy, perhaps.

> **For Example**
> I have a friend, when after I asked her to stop yelling at me, told me that she is Italian. Italians, evidently, when they get excited about something start yelling. But I'm not supposed to interpret this information negatively: the yelling should be seen as positive, excited enthusiasm.

But you shouldn't believe me just because I'm saying it, so let's test it in a syllogism:

Syllogism #22
(1) Consider cleaning their rooms,
(2) My children will do it,
(3) Because I yelled at them.

True or not true? You should know the drill by now; the only way to be sure is to run the tests. Or maybe common sense is good enough. I don't know; let's check.

Test #1: Is there a relationship between the (1) subject (cleaning their rooms) and the (3) reason (because I yelled at them)?

Yes, you yelled at your children to clean their rooms. So that's how they apply.

But let's run the second test, because by now, you should be catching on to the fact that this is where most of these kinds of arguments fail. And this is really important—if you can think of an exception to test #2, then the syllogism fails, because there's no positive necessity. So try to start training your mind to look for these kinds of exceptions. Remember, if you can find just one exception to test #2, the syllogism must be false.

Test #2: If the (3) reason ("Because yelling is a way to make sure things get done") is true, then the (2) thing you're trying to prove *must always* be true ("It will get them to do what I want").

True or false? You have to say that's false. Again, it only takes one counter example to prove that there is no positive necessity. So if you can think of a time when yelling at the kids didn't get them to do what you wanted, this syllogism is not true.

Does that mean you should never yell at your kids? I'm not saying that. If one of your children is running out in the street and might get hit by a car, you better yell at them, because that will plant a seed of protecting life. Just be aware that if they do stop, it's not because you yelled at them, and only because you listened to what someone else asked you to do before.

And for the sake of completeness (and in order to practice negation), what is test #3?

Test #3: If we negate the (2) assertion, the (3) reason must also be negated.

So if you don't yell at them, does that mean that your children won't clean their rooms? Is it also possible to not yell at them and they might still clean their rooms? (Hint: maybe you could bribe them?) As unlikely as it may seem, you have to say that's possible—and so again, this syllogism is false.

Exercises

1. Is the reason, "Because not yelling at them won't solve my problems" positive or negative?

2. What about the reason, "Because it's not possible that the thing doesn't exist." Is it positive or negative?

3. And finally, what about the assertion, "It's definitely not true that just because a thing is empty it doesn't exist." Is it positive or negative?

Chapter 12: Proof of Emptiness

Okay, but maybe you don't believe all of this. Up to this point, we've made some assumptions, so let's take a look at some of them. Can we prove the ideas we're talking about without relying on any assumptions?

If you've taken a philosophy class before, and/or have studied mathematics or the philosophy of numbers, and think you have other assumptions I haven't discussed, please see the Appendix F, "Assumptions."

There are many, many proofs for emptiness, but we're going to boil them all down into three groups: the emptiness of subjects and objects, the emptiness of causes and results, and the emptiness of changing (functioning) and unchanging things.

For those of you with a logical or a mathematical background, these three groups are not exclusive categories.

The most important proof for emptiness in the Tibetan wisdom tradition is called "The King of Reasons." First, however, let's start with the one we gave before:

<u>Syllogism #23</u>
(1) Consider my pen,
(2) It's empty,
(3) Because a dog sees it as something to chew on.

Okay, is this one true or false? Hopefully you know what to do by now: we have to run the three tests.

Test #1: Is the pen that I see something a dog might chew on? Yes, according to my dog, this applies.

Test #2: If the dog doesn't see a pen, but instead sees something to chew on, does that mean the pen must be empty?

Again, yes, this is what emptiness means: the object is empty of being, by itself, what you thought it was. So if the pen was somehow a pen, a pen from its own side, if it had penness to it, if it was a pen by itself, then the dog would have to see a pen. But they don't. So we can say the pen is empty of being a pen; in other words, the idea "pen" is coming from me.

Test #3: If the pen were not empty, if it were a pen from its own side, would a dog not see it as something to chew on; that is, would it see it as a pen?

Again, this is just the reverse, but it's good to think in terms of negation! So think about it: if I held up my pen to a dog, and she took it from me and started writing with it, would that mean that the pen wasn't empty? Yes, that would mean that the pen would be coming from its own side. If anyone who looked at it was forced to see it as a pen, and no one could see it as something different, then you would have found a self-existent thing, and it would not be empty. You would have found the object that emptiness denies.

In the Tibetan wisdom tradition, this is a critically important thing to understand: if emptiness is negation, then it has to deny something. What is the thing that emptiness denies? That a thing could ever be the thing that it is by itself.

Okay, so what if we remove the dog? You and I would agree that my pen is a pen. Does that somehow invalidate the idea

> ⓘ *The process by which this is happening is discussed in Chapter 8, "The Key to It All."*

of emptiness? No, because consensus is not a proof. If we all agree the moon *is* made out of cheese, does that transform it into cheese? In other words, to reverse the process doesn't work.

Let's try another one. Here we'll play with the idea that cause and effect relationships are also empty. Remember: emptiness doesn't mean that things don't work.

In fact, something can only work if it's empty. If something could come from its own side, independent of how we saw it—if it was coming from itself, self-powered—then it could not change. For something to work, it has to change from one thing to another.
Think about it.

Instead, emptiness just means that things don't work the way we thought they did—that is, coming from themselves and that somehow they have the power to work independently of how we have treated others in the past.

<u>Syllogism 24</u>
(1) Consider a day,
(2) You can't experience one,
(3) Because a day must consist of a morning, an afternoon, and an evening.

True or false? Could it be that our experience of a day is also empty? Let's check:

Test #1: Does a day consist of a morning, an afternoon, and an evening?

Test #2: If a day must consist of a morning, an afternoon, and an evening, does that mean you can't experience one?

What do you think? Can you experience a morning and an evening at the same time? If not, how can you ever experience a day?

The truth is you can't, self-existently. You can experience a day (okay, this syllogism is false, it's just meant to make you think), just not the way you thought you did. The only way you ever experienced a day was that your mind drew a circle around a bunch of disparate parts—a morning, an afternoon, and an evening—and labeled it as a "day."

Think about it: how does a morning resemble an evening? What do they have in common? Does the sun ever rise during an evening? Or the sun go down during a morning? And if they don't have much in common, why do you lump them together into something called a "day"?

Okay, so let's redo it to make it correct:

<u>Syllogism 25</u>
(1) Consider a day,
(2) It's empty,
(3) Because you can't experience a morning and an evening at the same time.

Test #1: Does a day share a relationship with a morning and an evening? Yes, it's dependent on those parts: you can't experience a day without them.

Test #2: If you can't experience a morning and an evening at the same time, does that mean a day must be empty?

Yes, a day is no thing other than a projection on disparate parts forced on you by how you've planted seeds in the past. There's no similarity between a morning and an evening—the only way you see a connection is that your mind created one.

> *We can use the dog example as well. We see a "day," but does a dog ever think to himself at the end of that day, "Wow, that was a great day! I hope tomorrow is the same!"*

Test #3: If a day weren't empty, could you experience a morning and an evening at the same time?

Now we're getting really deep; that's too abstract for me. So let's go back to something more concrete first. That is, if you were experiencing a self-existent day, coming from its own side, could you experience both a morning and an evening simultaneously? You would have to.

Exercise

Consider this syllogism and then answer the following questions.

<u>Syllogism #26</u>
(1) Consider my ex-girlfriend/boyfriend,
(2) They're empty,
(3) Because although I/others dislike them, they also have friends.

1. What is the subject, assertion, and reason?

2. What is the first test in this case? (Use this example in your answer.)

3. What is the second test? (Use this example in your answer.)

4. What is the third test? (Use this example in your answer.)

5. Is this syllogism true or false?

Chapter 13: The True Cause of Relationships

So we've also had this one before:

Syllogism #10
(1) Consider the girl/guy of my dreams,
(2) I will meet her/him,
(3) Because I'm using an executive dating service.

Didn't we decide this one is false? If you don't remember how, go back and review chapter five. But basically, using an executive dating service doesn't mean you must meet the girl (or guy) of your dreams. So how do we fix this one?

Syllogism #27
(1) Consider the girl of my dreams,
(2) I will meet her,
(3) Because I bring people together.

So let's run the tests.

Test #1: Is there a relationship between the girl of my dreams and my bringing people together? Yes, bringing people together is the seed to meet her.

Test #2: If I bring people together, *must* I meet the girl of my dreams?

Yes, if the law of seeds #1 is true; if seeds are definite then the result of bringing people together is that I must meet someone.

Okay, so we assumed before that the laws of seeds are true. Now can we prove them?

> ⓘ *Again, if you need to review the four laws of seeds please see Appendix B, "The Four Laws of Seeds."*

To really do this would be another whole book, but here's the gist: as Sherlock Holmes first taught me, if you eliminate all the other possibilities, what is left must be the truth. So what are the possibilities?

Well, the possibilities are infinite, but we can collect them all into a group of three: God makes everything happen, everything is random, or things obey the laws of cause and effect. I think what you'll find, if you think about it, is that every explanation for why things happen will fit into some version of one of these three possibilities.

 *Or all three. One of my friends likes to joke, "When something good happens to me it's cause and effect. When something bad happens, it's random (s@#t happens). And when you really need something, well, everybody knows there are no atheists in foxholes."*

Nobody really accepts the first position, because there's an inherent logical contradiction in it. If we define God as a loving being (what religion doesn't?), then we have to believe that God is not making everything happen. Why? Because I feel pain, and what loving God would make me go through that?

<u>Syllogism #28</u>
(1) Consider God,
(2) He is not omnipotent,
(3) Because I feel pain.

Either one of two possibilities is true: either God (if he or she exists) is omnipotent and cruel, or they are loving and not omnipotent. How do we know? Run the tests.

Test #1: Is it true that I feel pain? If so, does an omnipotent God therefore allow it? (Or even worse, actually cause it?) If I feel pain, and God is the cause of it, then this syllogism passes test #1.

Test #2: If I feel pain, is God therefore not omnipotent? Yes, because a loving God, if he or she were omnipotent, would not allow me to be in pain.

If I'm a compassionate person, and I see someone in pain, can I stand by and watch without doing anything? Or actually here, in this case, can I lovingly inflict pain? When all along I had the power to stop it? Or must it be as Shakespeare said, "As flies to wanton boys are we to th' Gods/They kill us for their sport."

> *The most important thing, before you debate with someone, is to agree on your terms. If you want to debate about God, first you have to decide what you mean by "God." Is God the old, bearded man in the sky that causes everything to happen? If so, there are some logical problems with that. If by God, however, you mean a divine presence that guides you in you life, well, that's a different story.*

It's not my purpose here to cause a crisis of faith for anyone. Philosophers and religious mystics have asked this question for millennia, and the most common answer I've heard is, "It's a mystery." That's fine, if that's a good enough answer for you. But logically, it doesn't work. You can say, "Okay, they allow us to feel pain so we can learn." But if God is omnipotent, then why?

Why not just create me with the information I need? Why torture me first? To help me? What kind of sick mind would think that way?

Again, it's not my purpose to disprove God. In fact, I have plans to write out a formal proof for the existence of divine beings. But I can't accept that they're omnipotent (or that they don't change), because logically that just doesn't work.

Okay, so let's look at option #2: it's all random. Just molecules and electrons and quarks whizzing around at the speed of light, crashing into each other—and this created me, my likes and dislikes, my loves, my sadness, my pain: everything I am and feel.

Yeah, sure, it's possible. So let's test it out:

<u>**Syllogism #29**</u>
(1) Consider the world,
(2) It's random,
(3) Because anything can happen.

Sounds good right? I almost agree with it myself. But let's test it.

Test #1: In the world, anything can happen, right?

On a certain level, I think it's great to think like this. The Buddha said that we can stop birth, old age, sickness, and death.

>  *Again, really, I'm not trying to make you Buddhist: pray or don't pray to whomever you want. I personally think Jesus and Buddha were mostly saying the same thing, anyway. Why do you think Jesus told us to turn the other cheek?*

As in, no one would have to die anymore. We could live in a world where no one gets sick and no one dies. To accept this logically, all you have to do is accept cause and effect. If death exists, must it have a cause? Then, if you remove that cause, you must remove the result. So assuming it's possible to stop the cause, it's inevitable that you would stop the effect.

So on that level, I want to say, "Yes, anything is possible." But is it literally true that anything is possible? Do you really believe that in the next moment, it could start raining rabbits? Or that leprechauns might show up and steal all your money?

Do you send your kids to school? Why? It's random whether they would learn anything or not. Do you go to work? Why? Whether you get paid or not is only random, you could just as easily get paid waiting for a bus. Why aren't you at the bus stop?

If you're going to logically hold the view that all things are random, then you have to follow this line of thinking out to its logical consequences. If everything were random, you wouldn't plan anything, or work towards anything, or try to do anything actually, because the result of whatever it was that you planned, worked towards, or did would be totally random. Nobody really believes that, and logically it doesn't make any sense either.

So what's left? Things must be the result of cause and effect.

I want to point out one other thing here; we already said that it's difficult to identify the cause of something because of the time gap— because of the time gap we can't see, immediately, what is going to result from our actions.

But given the time gap, how do I know what the real cause for something was? Sometimes, to find the right cause (that is, the

> ⓘ *Again, I don't have the space here to really go into this, but you can visit our website at easytibetanlogic.com for more information about how to figure out what the cause for something is.*

right seed) for something, you have to be like a scientist and investigate.

I always tell the story about how I had a boss who criticized me. I was confused, because I didn't think I was doing anything that I should be criticized for. So I thought, "I must be planting a seed that is causing this." So I decided to try to fix it by not planting the seed for criticism: I stopped criticizing others.

But after a few days I checked, and I wasn't criticizing anyone else, but this man was still criticizing me. So I thought, the seed must be something else.

For example, why are you interested in finding a partner? Remember, the first law of seeds says the result must be similar. (You can't get carrots from watermelon seeds). So what are you interested in? For example, if you're feeling lonely, what you should do is help a lonely person. Go visit an elderly person at a nursing home. I've gone; they're desperate for any kind of human interaction. Or you could visit an orphanage, or in some other way take care of children who are lonely. This would plant the seed for you to not be lonely.

But the Yoga Sutra says that the seed—the real cause—to meet the angel of your wildest dreams is study (specifically, studying spiritual ideas). So you could do any of these: visit an elderly person in a nursing home, or visit an orphanage, or read a book about emptiness. Any of these things could be the cause for you to meet a spiritual partner; all of them would be good ways to plant the seed.

Similarly, the seed to find a business partner or a new employee is to help other people find the talent they are looking for. For example, if you hear your friend is looking for work, and someone else could use their skills, try to connect them. But this seed could apply to romantic relationships as well: if someone hits on you, and you're not feeling it, don't just blow them off (unless you want the angel of your wildest dreams to do that to you); try to set them up with someone else you know, if you think it might work out. Or, if you can't do that, then at the very least wish them good luck.

Remember, the point of this discussion is that the result must resemble the cause; that is, the seed you planted must have come from something you did that was similar. So if you're thinking to yourself, "How did that happen?" it must be because you did something similar before; it's not random, and you can't blame God.

So let's go back to syllogism #27 and finish the last test. (You thought I forgot, didn't you?)

Test #3: Is it true that if I don't meet the girl of my dreams, I didn't bring people together?

Yes, you'll never meet them if you spend your time splitting people apart, because the seed of splitting people apart (dividing them with your actions or speech) is that you'll always see everyone fighting. So if you want to meet the angel of your dreams and argue with them, then by all means, talk badly about the people around you.

By the way, this is also very important for people working in business. If you spend time talking badly about others to your friends, the result is you will see people around you fighting with each other—something that doesn't really support much work getting done.

Exercises

Consider this syllogism and then answer the following questions.

<u>Syllogism #30</u>
(1) Consider the guy/girl of my dreams,
(2) I will meet them,
(3) Because I'm asking my friends to set me up/I spend a lot of time at the bars/I'm beautiful/very generous/easy-going.

1. What is the first test in this case? (Use this example in your answer.)

2. What is the second test? (Use this example in your answer.)

3. What is the third test? (Use this example in your answer.)

4. Are these syllogisms true or false? If they're false, write out one that's true (passes the three tests.)

Chapter 14: Another Proof for Emptiness

So let's do another proof for emptiness. We've given an arguments for why objects are empty and for why results are empty. So let's maybe try one for why causes are empty.

<u>Syllogism #31</u>
(1) Consider a sprout,
(2) It doesn't come from a seed,
(3) Because they never touch.

Interesting. So how does this one work out?

Test #1: "They" refers to both the seed and the sprout, so the subject applies to the reason. But is the reason factually correct?

> ⓘ *Remember, if something is not true, it doesn't exist—and things that don't exist can't share a relationship with anything else.*

That is, do a seed and the sprout that comes after it ever exist at the same time? No, that's impossible. The seed and sprout can't exist at the same time; that is, in the same moment. If they could, for example, then there would be two things, not one.

So if they don't exist at the same time then they can't touch, since one or the other would not be present in the same moment. How could a seed touch a sprout that doesn't exist yet, or a sprout touch a seed that must be gone by then? They couldn't.

Test #2: If two things never touch, can one cause the other?

Again, if they never touch then one could never cause the other. Could you pick up a pen without touching it? Could I type this book out without touching the keyboard?

Test #3: If a sprout did come from a seed, would they have to touch?

Yes, for the seed to affect the sprout it would have to be able to touch it.

Right now you're probably feeling confused. How does a sprout not come from a seed?

Of course they do. But again, just not the way you thought they did: a seed cannot self-existently touch a sprout, nor is a seed the cause of the sprout. How else do we know this is true? In the next chapter we'll look at another proof for emptiness: the emptiness of how things work.

Exercises

Consider this syllogism and then answer the following questions.

<u>Syllogism #32</u>
(1) Consider a pen,
(2) It does not come from a pen factory (the pen factory is not the cause of the pen),
(3) Because my dog sees it as something to chew on.

1. What is the first test in this case? (Use this example in your answer.)

2. What is the second test? (Use this example in your answer.)

3. What is the third test? (Use this example in your answer.)

4. Is this syllogism true or false? Write out your own proof for emptiness using the idea that apparent causes are also empty.

Chapter 15:
The Emptiness of How Things Work

So we've discussed the emptiness of objects and the emptiness of causes and results. So let's work on the emptiness of changing (functioning) things.

<u>Syllogism #33</u>
(1) Consider an aspirin,
(2) It isn't the cause of removing your headache,
(3) Because it doesn't work every time.

Test #1: We refer here to aspirin both in the subject and reason, so the subject applies to the reason as long as the reason is true: do or don't aspirins work every time? My experience is that they don't.

Test #2: If something doesn't work to produce its result every time, could it be the cause?

So this is the important part. By definition, to be a cause, that thing has to produce a result. If it doesn't, in what sense is it a cause? That is, to be a cause, it has to *cause* something.

So if a cause has to cause something, it should cause that thing (the result) every time. If it doesn't, then you haven't found the real cause—just a correlation or something that just looks like the cause.

Remember the third law of seeds says that if the seed is planted the result must come. Scientists agree with this, but where they struggle to control external circumstances and engage in double blind studies hoping to show a consistent result, the Tibetan wisdom tradition says simply identify the true cause for what you want (meaning the mental seed) and the external circumstances will work themselves out.

For example, let's say I have migraine headaches. Should I try expensive treatments or take drugs tested through rigorous research studies? Will one work? Both? Neither?

That should sound familiar to you by now; it's the three or four possibilities game. What do you think? Is it three or four possibilities? If you know someone who took drugs and it worked, or someone who used alternative treatments, or someone who used both, or someone for whom neither worked, then what have you got? You've identified there's no real cause and effect relationship between these things.

So if an aspirin is not the cause of removing my headache (even when it looks like it does), what is the real cause?

<u>Syllogism #34</u>
(1) Consider an aspirin,
(2) It will cure your headache,
(3) Because you have the seed for it to work.

If you don't have the seed for an aspirin to work, you can take as many of them as you want and all you'll get is an ulcer.

I think it's interesting that substances designated as "medicines" can often hurt us. How does something that's supposed to improve your health hurt you? Have you ever read the warning label on aspirin? It's terrifying. The fact is that medicines are empty like everything else; they don't have the power, from themselves, to help you. They will only work if you have planted the seed for them to work by having been kind to others in the past.

But let's run the tests to be sure.

Test #1: Do you have the seed for an aspirin to work?

Test #2: If you have the seed for an aspirin to work, must it cure your headache? (What law of seeds covers this?)

Test #3: If it doesn't cure your headache, does that mean you must not have had the seed for it to work? In other words, if it doesn't work is it because you didn't have the cause in place for the aspirin to work?

So you have to think about this. If the purpose of an aspirin is to remove headaches, but it doesn't, why is that? Scientists will do all kinds of studies and examine your brain chemistry (which is great; I don't mean to say they shouldn't) and might find some chemical reason in your brain why the aspirin didn't work. But for our purposes, we don't care—because if the aspirin doesn't work sometimes, that means it's not really the cause. It's just a vehicle—a way for the mental seed in your mind to express itself. If you don't think so, play the three or four possibilities game and check for yourself.

Exercises

1. List the four laws of seeds.

2. Write out test #3 for syllogism #34.

3. Write out a syllogism for a successful pregnancy. What reason would you give?

Chapter 16:
Getting things to Work, Part Two

So we know now how to get medicine to work. What about something mechanical like starting your car?

<u>Syllogism #35</u>
**(1) Consider my car,
(2) It will start,
(3) Because I'm turning the key.**

So is this one true or false? By now maybe you can start to see how these are going to work: this one is false, because your car doesn't start every time you turn the key. (Which test is that? That is, which test does this syllogism fail?)

Now you're thinking, "But it's not the key's fault! I didn't have gas/the distributor wasn't working/ it needed a tune-up!" But again, you're missing the point: the cause *must* produce the result. No amount of repairs will get the car going if you don't have the seed for it to work. (Your insurance company will total the car, or the mechanic won't be able to find a part, or will continue to find more problems, and so on and so on).

<u>**Syllogism #36**</u>
(1) Consider my stove,
(2) It will cook my dinner,
(3) Because that's its purpose.

What about this one? Is it true or false? Just because the reason why you bought a stove was to make dinner, will that keep it from burning you? Or if you have a gas stove, from even killing you?

Things only work if you plant the right seed for them to work. Otherwise, anything can happen, because stoves, like anything else, are empty.

For Example
How does an ant running across your stove experience it when you turn it on? What is the ant thinking, "Great, now he'll make my dinner"? Or does he see his own fiery imminent death? For you a stove is a way to make your dinner, but to an ant it's only danger, because the stove itself, from its own side, is neither something that can make your dinner nor something dangerous. It's empty of being those things, and will only appear to you that way if you have the seed for it to be one of them.

Exercises

1. Which test does the syllogism #35 fail?

2. Write out test #3 for the syllogism #35.

3. Write out test #2 for syllogism #36.

4. Write out a correct syllogism for how you will get your dinner. (I'll give you a hint; you'll have to write out the real cause for getting it.)

Chapter 17:
The King of Reasons

Okay, we're getting close to the end. (You survived! Your t-shirt is in the mail.) You basically know everything now to start working things out for yourself. (Should I take the promotion? Am I ready to get married? Have kids? What do I do about my mother-in-law?) But we'll cover a few more details. Take a break, have something to drink, then read more only if you're interested.

So we covered how changing things are empty, but what about unchanging things?

> *Changing things are functioning things are working things; they are all synonyms. If something works, it did something—and had to change to do so.*

The classic example to use in Tibetan logic is space. In Tibetan philosophy, space is not the distance between two objects, nor is it the blackness of outer space. Here we define space as placeholder; that is, space is the place that something occupies. It can be either occupied or not occupied, but it doesn't change. If it did, then when that space was occupied it couldn't hold the object that is there. (Okay, you might have to think about that for a while. Don't worry about it.) In other words, when something moves through a space it doesn't change the space, because the space that is occupied is always the place that an object can occupy.

So if everything is empty, then space is also something that has to be empty.

If everything is empty, then so is emptiness itself—for more on this see Appendix G, "Even Emptiness must be Empty."

But how do we prove it? If changing things do not change, then they cannot do anything (that is, work or function). So we can't use some of the reasons above, because they only apply to things that change or do something.

Instead we'll use the reason I mentioned before that Tibetans call the "King of Reasons." The basic format of the King of Reasons is:

Syllogism #37
(1) Consider some thing,
(2) It is empty,
(3) Because it depends on something else.

Something else like what? For one thing, everything depends on your mind conceiving of it the way that you do. The idea here is that if something exists from its own side, that is, from its own power, then it can't depend on something else. In our pen example, the pen is not a pen from its own side, because to see it as a pen depends on us seeing it as a pen. It doesn't have the power to appear as a pen by itself. That is, since the dog doesn't see long, thin, and black as a pen, then that object requires us—depends on us—seeing it as a pen in order for it to be a pen. Remember, the eyeball itself can only see shape and color. It can't see "pen," which is an idea or a concept that dogs don't understand.

But let's try using another example. There are lots of ways in which things depend on other things. And anything that depends on something else is empty, because if that thing depends on something else then it doesn't come from itself.

Consider:

<u>Syllogism #38</u>
(1) Consider space,
(2) It's empty,
(3) Because it depends on parts.

So let's run the tests to see if this is true.

Test #1: Is it true that space depends on parts?

In Tibetan philosophy we say yes: everything has parts. Think about any physical thing. It has to have parts: top, bottom, left, right, front, and back.

>  *Coincidently, this is also why scientists will never find a smallest particle. Any particle they find must have a front and back, left and right, top and bottom. And if this is true, no matter how small it is, that particle can be split into parts. And guess what? It will have to have parts as well. Can a particle, no matter how tiny it is, exist without a top?*

No matter how small it is, or how large, it must have a front and back, bottom and top.

So all physical things have parts. What about mental things (mainly thoughts and awareness of those thoughts)? Do they have parts? Well, as we said before, thoughts exist in time, and so anything that exists over time can be split into parts; it must have a beginning, a middle, and an end. Or you can think of that object as it exists in series of moments; that is, any object in moment t, moment t+1, moment t+2, and so on.

So what are the parts of space? Up, down, left right, forward, and backward.

Don't believe me? You can check. We'll learn how to do that in the next chapter.

Exercises

1. Write out the syllogism for the King of Reasons using your own example.

2. Write out tests #1, #2, and #3 for syllogism #37, the King of Reasons.

3. Write out tests #1, #2, and #3 for syllogism #38.

Chapter 18: Following Up on a Syllogism

In Tibetan logic, if you don't accept a syllogism (or if your debate partner doesn't) then it's not over. You can't just say, "No, I think you're wrong." Then you're just giving your opinion. If a syllogism is false, you have to be able to prove it. And if it's not, we should be able to show that also. So put your logic hat on; here we go.

The structure of how to follow up with a response depends on which test the syllogism fails. So take our first example:

<u>Syllogism #1</u>
(1) Consider a Ford Mustang,
(2) It's a car,
(3) Because I like monkeys.

Which test does this syllogism fail? If you don't remember, go back and review chapter two.

Otherwise, obviously there's no relationship between Mustangs and monkeys (other than the fact that I just made an alliteration), so it fails test #1.

If a syllogism fails test #1, in Tibetan logic, you reply, "Your reason is not established." But be careful though; this doesn't necessarily mean there is anything wrong with the reason. What it means is the reason does not apply to this particular subject. I do like monkeys; that statement is true. It just doesn't have anything to do with Mustangs.

But if someone tells you, "Your reason is not established," and you think that they are wrong (your syllogism is correct), then what you do is make a new syllogism: your (3) old reason becomes your (2) new assertion and you make a new reason and keep going.

So, for example, with syllogism #1 above, if someone tells you your reason is not established (again, meaning your subject does not apply to your reason), you might say:

<u>Syllogism #39</u>
(1) Consider a Ford Mustang,
(2) It is like a monkey,
(3) Because they both start with the letter "m."

I'm being silly (at the risk of losing you), but the idea is that in the beginning logic should be fun; it's just a game. It's not a boring, useless thing like your high school math classes: it can be fun and exciting! (For more on this, please see Appendix D, "Sillygisms.)

But seriously (or more significantly), let's go back to our debate about space. For example, if you say:

<u>Syllogism #40</u>
(1) Consider space,
(2) It's empty,
(3) Because it depends on parts.

And your debate partner responds, "Your reason is not established," what would you do next? Here, what they would be saying is that there is no relationship between space and that fact that it has parts (no relationship between "space" and "it [space] having parts"). Which is to say

> (i) You've heard all this before; if you don't remember, go back and look at chapter 17.

that they would be saying space doesn't have parts. If space does not have parts, then there can be no relationship between space and the fact "space has parts," because no such fact exists—a non-existing thing can't share a relationship with anything else.

So how would you respond? Take the (3) old reason and make it your (2) new assertion and then come up with a (3) new reason.

For example:

<u>Syllogism#41</u>
(1) Consider space,
(2) It does depend on parts,
(3) Because space couldn't exist without having an up and down, left and right, and front and back.

And if your friend responds again, "Your reason is not established." Then what would you do? The same thing: take the (3) old reason and make it your (2) new assertion and then come up with a (3) new reason. For example:

<u>Syllogism#42</u>
(1) Consider space,
(2) It is so true that it couldn't exist without having an up and down, left and right, and front and back,
(3) Because there is no thing that exists that way.

And you can keep going until both people are satisfied. That is, if they say your reason is not established again, you would just keep repeating the same procedure.

Exercises

1. Run the tests on syllogism #41. Does it pass or fail (is it true or false)?

2. Assume your debate partner again answers, "Your reason is not established" after you give them syllogism #42. What would you do next?

Chapter 19: Not Necessarily, My Friend

We covered what to do if a syllogism fails (or someone thinks it fails) the first test. What do we do if a syllogism fails the second or third test? First, your answer now is, "Not necessarily." That tells the person giving the syllogism that you think their syllogism fails the second or third test, rather than the first (or you would have said, "Your reason is not established"). Let's use syllogism #2 as an example again:

<u>Syllogism #2</u>
(1) Consider a Ford Mustang,
(2) It is a car,
(3) Because it exists.

What test does this one fail? If you can't figure it out, go back and review chapter 3. Otherwise, just because something exists doesn't mean that it has to be a car. So it fails test #2. If a syllogism fails test #2 in Tibetan logic then your answer is, "Not necessarily." Meaning, it's not true that just because something exists it necessarily has to be a car.

So we learned in the last chapter how to follow up if a syllogism fails test #1. Now we'll learn how to follow up if a syllogism fails test #2. What happens next is you have to prove the necessity of what you said. So:

(1) It is true that because something exists it must be a car, because...

Good luck with that one.

That one is false, so let's try one that's true:

Syllogism #43
(1) Consider a sound,
(2) It's not red,
(3) Because it's not a color.

If your partner says, "Not necessarily," then what would you say? Maybe something like:

Syllogism #44
(1) It is so the case that if something is not a color it must not be red,
(2) Because if you take away all colors you must take away the color red.

And then, like before, you keep going until both people are satisfied that you've found the right answer.

Exercises

1. If this were your original syllogism:

<u>Syllogism #15</u>
**(1) Consider money,
(2) I'm going to get some,
(3) Because I give it away.**

And your debate partner answered, "Not necessarily," what does that mean? Use the syllogism in your answer.

2. If they answered as above, how would you respond? Give a new syllogism.

3. Which law is it (of the four laws) that says that if you give something away you must get something in return?

Chapter 20:
Conclusion and
Encouragement to Continue

So now you know everything you need to know to use logic to make better decisions in your life. My teacher told me, "Everyone in the morning gets up, and they put their feet on the floor, because they want something." The problem is, we all suffer, because sometimes we don't get the things we want. And why is that? Because our reasons are wrong. I get up in the morning, because I think I have to go to work to make money; I think that I will make money if I go to work. Not necessarily. So when I get fired, or laid off, or I don't get my Christmas bonus, what happens? I get upset, unhappy. Why? Because I had a false expectation, set up by a bad logical thought process.

Now, instead, using the Tibetan wisdom tradition, you can work out the real reason why something works.

Go to work because at work you can plant the seeds to get the things you want. What do you do at work except help others?

If "time is money," what seeds are you planting by giving your time? There's a lot more to think about here, but that's for another time. But think about it: at work you are helping your employer, your co-workers, your customers, everyone. How many seeds is that?

Every happiness comes from helping others. So let's look at one last syllogism:

<u>Syllogism #45</u>
(1) Consider happiness,
(2) I will reach it,
(3) Because I will plant the seed for happiness by helping others.

So please, get up, go to work, exercise, and meet new people. But do it for the right reasons, don't set yourself up to fail by using mistaken ones. Everything you want is possible. Just figure out the correct cause, prove it to yourself, and you can reach your every goal.

Exercises

1. Write down what you want in life; what would make you happy.

2. Write it out as a syllogism; how are you going to make it happen?

3. Run the three tests; is your syllogism true? How do you know?

Appendix A: The Three Tests

For quick reference, here is a one-page summary of the three tests that determine if a syllogism is true:

Test #1: 1 & 3
Is there a relationship between the (1) subject and the (3) reason?

Test #2: If 3, then 2
If the (3) reason is true, then the (2) assertion *must* be true

Test #3: If not 2, then not 3
If you negate the assertion, then the (3) reason *must* also be negated

For example:

> **(1) Consider sound,**
> **(2) It's unchanging,**
> **(3) Because it's made.**

Test #1: Is sound something that is made?

Test #2: If something is made, must it be unchanging?

Test #3: If something is not unchanging (changing), must it be that it also was not made?

Appendix B: The Four Laws of Seeds

The Four Laws of Seeds

1. Seeds are definite (actions produce similar consequences).

2. Seeds increase (consequences are greater than their actions).

3. If you don't plant the seed, you can't get a result (you cannot meet a consequence if you haven't committed an action).

4. If you plant the seed, you must get a result (once an action is committed, the consequence cannot be lost).

First Law of Seeds: Seeds are Definite

The first law of seeds says that seeds are definite: that is, grapes don't come from thorns or figs from thistles. Or in other words, you get what you pay for: if you hurt someone, pain will come back to you. And if you are kind to someone, kindness will come back to you.

In Tibetan logic, we say a logical (deductive) perception should not invalidate a direct perception; that is, they should agree. For example, if your eyes tell you the apple is red, but the syllogism you've worked out says the apple should be green, then you've got a problem. Now, we have trouble believing this first law, because we think we see the opposite: I said something nice to him, but he said something nasty back to me. Or I gave her some money, and she never gave me anything. So my direct perception invalidates these laws, right?

No, we covered this back in chapter 6: the problem is that cause and effect doesn't work that way—I cannot see the result of my action in the moment I commit it. Seeds take time to ripen; I wouldn't plant an apple seed in the ground and expect an apple in the next moment. Similarly, if we give money we won't see the result of that right away. Does the fact that you don't see an apple the second after you plant the seed somehow prove that apples don't come from apple seeds?

The laws of seeds say that eventually this is what will happen: if I give away money, that plants a seed in my mind. Then that seed matures and eventually ripens (we'll get to that), and we do experience something nice coming back to us. This is an inescapable law.

The Second Law of Seeds: Seeds increase

The second law of seeds says that the results of what you get are larger than what you did. To use the seed analogy, how large is an apple seed and how big is the tree that results from it? How many apples are possible from a tree that grew from one small seed?

So the results from mental seeds are similar. You make one small, nasty comment and then get a mean, nasty boss/stepmother/teenager that lasts for years. The second law of seeds says this is possible: small seed, big result.

Usually the objection to this is, "Well, if that's true, why don't I always see big results coming back to me?" ("I gave some money once and nothing came back.") The answer is you do, it just takes longer than you think. The problem with the time gap is *by the time the seed ripens we have probably forgotten what we did to cause that result*.

Or the other possibility is that you didn't plant the seed correctly. If I take an apple seed and throw it on the sidewalk, how many apples will I get back? If you want to be good at this, like any farmer knows, you have to learn how to plant seeds correctly. But learning how to plant seeds correctly is not the subject of this book, so we'll leave that for another time.

The Third Law of Seeds: Not Done, Not Experienced

The third law of seeds also fits our physical seeds analogy perfectly. Say you buy a flowerpot. Then you fill the pot with soil, add some water, and wait. Will you get a flower? Of course not, you forgot the seed!

Mental seeds are just the same. You can work and work and work, but if you don't plant the seeds to see little green square pieces of paper have value they won't. By definition, you can't get a result without creating the cause. So if we create the causes for what we want we'll get what we want; if we don't, we won't.

I was talking to someone once who told me, "Okay, this system isn't true, because my boss yells at me, and I've never yelled at him." I couldn't help it and started laughing, because I knew how he had planted the seed: what would you guess was the seed if I told you that he has five boys? I had just seen him yelling at his children that morning. So the truth is, you cannot get a result without planting the seed that causes it first.

It's important that we all agree though. Does the world operate by cause and effect?

Science says things operate by cause and effect. Could you build a something without materials? Can an atom exist without protons and electrons? But if you ask them why, then they say there's no reason. This is the same as saying there's no cause and effect. That is, it's not possible that things are both random and the world exists by cause and effect; in Tibetan logic, cause and effect and random are opposite: to be one is not the other. Let's write it out as a syllogism:

Syllogism #46
(1) Consider the world,
(2) The things in it are the result of cause and effect,
(3) Because the world is not random.

Okay, true or false? Run the tests.

Stephen Hawking in his book *A Brief History of Time* called the cause of the Big Bang a "singularity." A "singularity" in science is their way of saying, "We don't understand the cause and effect relationship here."

You know this: when you were five, someone in your family died. And you asked your mother, "Why did they die?" And she told you because they got cancer, or they didn't see the other car coming, or their heart was bad. Then what did you say? "Why?" And they told you it was because it was their time. And then what did you say? "Why?" And eventually they told you to shut up.

But Tibetan logic would say you were on to something. Like a scientist would (should) say, if you can't replicate the result you haven't found the cause. Does cancer kill everyone? Do car accidents always result in death? If not, then those things are not the real cause. What is the cause of death? You hurt someone else. The seed then can express itself in myriad ways: some people die in their sleep, some people die tragically, and some people die "accidentally."

There's a famous Indian Buddhist writer named "Angel of Peace." He wrote that if we are honest with ourselves, there are only three possibilities to explain why things happen: God makes everything happen, things are random, or things are the result of cause and effect. (Actually, what we usually think is a mix of all three: if something good happens, I made it happen; if something bad happens, I think it's an accident; and if I need something, well, everyone knows there are no atheists in foxholes.)

But we covered this back in chapter 13. Is God really making everything happen? No one really accepts this; if you did why would you go to work? If God wants you to have money, you will. And if he doesn't, you won't. Of course, God helps those who help themselves, but can you not do God's will, if he is making everything happen? You see the logical dilemma.

Again, I'm not saying there is no God. People have said that Buddhism says there is no God. That's not actually true; what's important is how you define what God is. For example, if you say that God is an uncreated creator; that's a problem. Because to create something requires that you be able to change. Changing and unchanging are opposites: to be one is not to be the other. You can't change things and also be unchanging; that's logically impossible. But that's not to say that God doesn't exist. If, for example, you believe in a divine being and think about them in the right way, what seed would that plant?

But I'm getting off the subject... let's talk about randomness again. Is the world random? Some people succeed, some people fail, some die in accidents, and some get lucky and live a dream life. Right?

But like we said before, if you believed this you wouldn't go to school or send your kids to school. Why would you? Everything is random. How would you remember what you learned from one day to the next? Whether you could or not would be totally random. You wouldn't go to work: whether you made money or your car got stolen, who could say?

The world can seem random, of course. But that's because we don't know what seeds we might have in our mind, like time bombs, waiting to go off. Which brings us to the last of the four laws of seeds.

The Fourth Law of Seeds: If You Do the Crime, You Pay the Time (Or, "Virtue Is Its Own Reward")

The last law of seeds in our discussion says that if you create the cause, you must get the result. To use our metaphor again, if you plant the seed correctly, the flower will grow. You don't have to worry if you're going to get an eggplant instead, or if flower seeds stopped growing this year—it's predictable.

This is even truer for mental seeds, because they are the real cause for what you're experiencing.

So does that mean there's nothing we can do? If I yell at my mother, must I see people yelling back at me?

This and the first law of seeds say, "Yes." But there is a caveat: again, mental seeds are like physical seeds, so similarly, they need the right conditions to grow. "A seed on rocky soil..." cannot grow. We talked about this before, but this explains why your mother isn't a millionaire: maybe she gave away a lot, but if she didn't plant her seeds correctly, then they won't grow well.

Similarly, for bad seeds, if we don't want to see them ripen, what we have to do is create rocky soil for them.

Again, this isn't the place, but basically rocky soil for a bad seed is the understanding of where things come from. Think about it: if you knew that yelling at someone was the cause for everyone who has ever yelled at you, would you keep yelling at people?

In fact, every time you yell at someone again it's like you're watering all the bad seeds of yelling you planted before. So you have to break the cycle; remember where things come from and behave accordingly. Then you will stop seeing all the things you dislike and start enjoying the world that you always dreamed of.

Exercises

1. What is the first law of seeds? Give an example of how this could work in your own life.

2. Write out a syllogism that uses the first law of seeds as a reason. (Consider x; y is true, because seeds are definite.)

3. What is the second law of seeds? Give an example of what this might look like in your own life.

4. Write out a syllogism that uses the second law of seeds as a reason. (Consider x; y is true, because seeds increase.)

5. What is the third law of seeds? Give an example of how this could work in your own life.

6. Write out a syllogism that uses the third law of seeds as a reason. (Consider x; y is true, because if you don't plant a seed you can't get a result.)

7. What is the fourth law of seeds? Give an example of how this could work in your own life.

8. Write out a syllogism that uses the fourth law of seeds as a reason. (Consider x; y is true, because a seed planted must have a result.)

Appendix C: Debating

In the big Tibetan Gelukpa monasteries they have a formalized way of practicing logic with a partner that we call debating. So when you go to debate (and everyone has to) you start off with two people: one is the attacker and one is the defender. The defender sits down and the attacker stands and asks questions. What is important is that both participants restrict themselves to the format: the attacker asks confirmation questions and presents syllogisms, and the defender is only allowed to respond with either yes and no (to confirmation questions) or "I agree," "Reason not established," and "Not necessarily" (to a syllogism).

I almost can't overemphasis the benefit I feel I've received from practicing debating. Debating is learning to think logically on the fly, and as a pedagogical tool, I'm not sure it has any equivalent. My teacher first told me, and then I experienced myself, where debating revealed an answer to something that your instructor then taught the next day in class. When you have this experience, you'll understand the value of debating as a learning tool.

(Also, negatively, if you ever mess up debating you'll never forget the mistake you made—and never make it again.)

So here I'll just give you a quick example, then go and try it yourself.

Attacker: So you can't tell me the cause for making money?

Defender: No, that's not true.

Attacker: So you can tell me the cause?

Defender: Yes.

Attacker: Okay, tell me!

Defender: Giving money to others.

Attacker: So giving money to others is the cause of making money?

Defender: Yes.

Attacker: Consider the money I gave to my cousin, it is *not* the real cause of making money, because I never got anything back from it!

Defender: Your reason is not established.

Attacker: So it's not true that I never got anything back?

Defender: Yes.

Attacker: Consider the money I gave to my cousin, it is so that I never got anything back from it, because there's no money in my bank account!

Defender: Not necessarily.

Attacker: So you're saying that just because there's no money in my bank account, that doesn't mean I necessarily didn't get anything back?

Defender: Yes.

Attacker: Give me an example.

Defender: Sure. You're forgetting the time gap. Just because there's no money in your bank account now doesn't mean you won't get anything back from having given money to your cousin. You have a seed in your mind, and when that seed ripens, you will definitely get some money back, because that's the fourth law of seeds.

So this is how they learn in the monastery; don't be afraid to be wrong. Prove that what you think you know is correct before you accept it as correct. If both participants approach it this way (not trying to be right, just trying to reach the truth) then both people gain something and everyone wins.

Appendix D: Sillygisms

In the big Tibetan Gelukpa monasteries, when they want to start the monks debating, one of the first subjects they teach is color. Why color? Because it's simple (or at least, you think so until you debate it): if you get confused debating emptiness, did you get confused because you don't understand the concept of emptiness or because you don't understand the logic process? If you start with color, then if you get confused it's because you don't understand the process of debating and not because you didn't understand the subject.

So similarly, when we started debating in English, two of my friends, Evan Osherow and Ben Kramer, developed a way of teaching debating they called "sillygisms." The idea is, start debating simple things like "how do you know your shoes are on your feet?" Again, the idea is to ingrain the logical debate process. After I teach a logic class, the students always ask me, "What do we do next?" Practice. Practice, practice, practice.

So here I've included some sillygisms to get you started. Once you understand the principles of logic and debating, then there is nothing but to do it. Practice, practice, practice. Then once you have the system ingrained, you can start to use it to work on more important ideas like emptiness, dependent origination, and the meaning of life.

Sillygism #1: Shoes
Consider your shoes,
They're shoes,
Because they're on your feet.

Sillygism #2: The Sun
Consider the sun,
It's orange,
Because it's not blue.

Sillygism #3: Your Favorite TV Show
Consider "Game of Thrones,"
It's the best show on television,
Because the writing is so good.

Sillygism #4: The Pen
Consider the pen,
It's a pen,
Because I can write with it.

Sillygism #5: The Pen II
Consider the pen,
It's a pen,
Because it's always been that way.

Sillygism #6: The Pen III
Consider the pen,
It's mine,
Because I bought it.

Sillygism #7: A Broken Cup
Consider the broken cup,
It's not my fault,
Because it was an accident.

Sillygism #8: Jobs
Consider losing my job,
It's a terrible turn of events,
Because I didn't expect it.

Sillygism #9: Opinions
Consider your opinion,
You are wrong,
Because I am right.

Sillygism #10: Who's Better?
Consider Apple,
They're better than Microsoft,
Because they invented the iPhone.

Then when you've practiced all these, and can do the three tests with your eyes closed, try writing your own sillygisms and run the tests. An easy example would be—we already did your favorite TV show—can you do your favorite movie/actor/actress/song/band and so on? After you're good at that, try to write out the ones that failed and fix them. Can you write out sillygism #1 so that it is true?

Obviously we're making a joke by calling them sillygisms, but I think what you'll find after you practice them is actually you can start to get into some very deep subjects: how do we know the things we think we know? Why do some people like something but I don't? What is the nature of the things we experience?

Then I won't have to twist your arm anymore to do your math homework; you'll do it because you enjoy it and can see the benefit of learning it. (Tell Peggy Sue for me.) Practice, practice, practice, and then enjoy!

Appendix E: Answer Key

Chapter 2

1. Think of some of the positive reasons for studying logic; go from general to specific (that is, starting with "It will improve my mind" or "It will help me think more clearly and solve problems better" down to "I'll be able to figure out how to solve that problem at work more efficiently").

Of course everyone's answers to this question will be different, and one of the purposes of the book is to give you these reasons, but as an example, I had a student from one of my logic classes once thank me afterwards. I asked him how he was doing, and he said, "Great, I'm in law school." He said he was having a great time as a lawyer because of his logic training: no one could beat him now in a debate.

I have a friend who thinks the best thing about learning to think logically is that she can see through marketing ploys. "This is the best!" or "Results guaranteed!" Are these kinds of claims true or false?

2. **Play the three or four possibilities game. Start with something simple, like "red" and "ball." Then try something more complex, such as "intelligent" and "rich" or "beautiful" and "has a great relationship."**

You could also try "jogging" and "health" or "intelligent" with "study." Then try "good" and something you like or "bad" and something you dislike. What you'll find is that they are all relationships of four, so there is no cause and effect between them. For example, what is the relationship between dating and meeting Mr./Ms. Right? So, do you know anyone who dated someone and did meet them? Do you know someone who dated and didn't? Do you know someone who never dated but did? Or finally, do you know someone who never dated and never did? If so, it's a relationship of four.

Chapter 3

Consider the following syllogism and answer the questions about it:

Syllogism #3
(1) Consider John,
(2) He is a human being,
(3) Because he's a doctor.

1. What is the subject of this syllogism?

The subject of any syllogism is always in the first line. So the subject of this syllogism is "John."

2. What is its assertion (the thing it's trying to prove)?

Its assertion is, "John is a human being."

3. What reason does it use?

"Because John is a doctor."

4. What is the first test in this case? (Use this example in your answer.)

The first test is: is there a relationship between the (1) subject and the (3) reason. So here, is it true that John is a doctor?

5. What is the second test? (Use this example in your answer.)

The second test is, "If the (3) reason is true must it be the case that the (2) assertion is true?" So here, test #2 is, "Must it be true that if someone is a doctor they must be a human being?"

Chapter 4

Consider the following syllogism and then try to answer the questions about it:

<u>Syllogism #7</u>
(1) Consider the stock market,
(2) I should invest in it,
(3) Because it's my best chance to get a good return.

1. What is the subject?

The subject of syllogism #7 is, "the stock market."

2. What is the assertion (the thing it's trying to prove)?

The assertion (the thing we're trying to prove) for syllogism #7 is, "I should invest in the stock market."

3. What is the reason?

The reason for syllogism #7 is, "because it's my best chance to get a good return."

4. What is the first test in this case? (Use this example in your answer.)

The first test is to show a relationship between the (1) subject and the (3) reason. So here the first test would be: is it true that "the stock market is my best chance to get a good return"?

5. What is the second test? (Use this example in your answer.)

The second test is to show positive necessity: if the (3) reason is true must the (2) assertion be true? So here that would mean, "If the stock market is my best chance for a good return, must I (should I definitely) invest in it?"

6. Is this syllogism true or false (does it pass both tests?)

Your "best chance" still means you could lose all your money (which means it's **not** the case that you definitely should invest in it). So false, because this syllogism fails test #2: even if the stock market is your best chance (and we could debate whether that's true or not) that still doesn't mean you have to invest in it (or that it's even a good idea).

Chapter 5

Consider the following syllogism and then try to answer the questions about it:

<u>Syllogism #9</u>
(1) Consider chemotherapy,
(2) It will remove my cancer,
(3) Because my doctor says it is my best option.

1. What is the subject?

The subject of syllogism #9 is, "chemotherapy."

2. What is the assertion?

The assertion (the thing we're trying to prove) for syllogism #9 is, "Chemotherapy will remove my cancer."

3. What is the reason?

The reason for syllogism #9 is, "Because my doctor says it's my best option."

4. What is the first test in this case? (Use this example in your answer.)

The first test is to show a relationship between the (1) subject and the (3) reason. So here the first test would be, "Is chemotherapy my best option acording to my doctor"?

5. What is the second test? (Use this example in your answer.)

The second test is to show positive necessity: if the (3) reason is true must the (2) assertion be true? So here that would mean, "If my doctor says chemotherapy is my best option, will it necessarily (must it) remove my cancer?"

6. Is this syllogism true or false (does it pass both tests?)

False, because even if your doctor tells you chemotherapy is your best option, that doesn't mean necessarily it will work for you. (Do the three or four possibilities game; I have a friend who cured her cancer doing chemo, one who still died, one who refused chemo and cured herself using alternative medicine, and one who refused chemo to die at home, peacefully.)

Chapter 6

Consider the following syllogism and then try to answer the questions about it:

Syllogism #12
(1) Consider red lipstick
(2) It will make me more attractive,
(3) Because the man I'm interested in will think it's sexy.

1. **What is the subject?**

   The subject here is "red lipstick."

2. **What is the assertion?**

   The assertion here is "[Red lipstick] will make me more attractive."

3. **What is the reason?**

   And the reason is, "Because the man I'm interested in will think it's sexy."

4. **What is the first test in this case? (Use this example in your answer.)**

   The first test is to show a relationship between the (1) subject and the (3) reason. So here the first test would be, "Is red lipstick something that the man I'm interested in will think is sexy?"

5. What is the second test? (Use this example in your answer.)

The second test is to show positive necessity. So here that would mean, "If the man I'm interested in thinks red lipstick is sexy, must that make me more attractive to him?"

6. Is this syllogism true of false?

False, because this one could fail either test. If he doesn't think red lipstick is sexy (maybe he prefers the "natural look"), it fails test #1. And either way it fails test #2: just because red lipstick might make you look sexy doesn't mean he must be more attracted to you. For example, maybe he thinks red lipstick at work isn't appropriate (if you work together) or maybe he equates sexy with slutty and that's a big turn-off for him. Maybe he's looking to settle down and wants a nice girl…

Chapter 7

Read the following syllogism and answer the questions:

Syllogism #14
(1) Consider a car,
(2) It's not a motorcycle,
(3) Because cars and motorcycles are not the same.

1. **Please write down the subject, assertion, and reason for this assertion.**

   The subject is "a car," the assertion is "a car is not a motorcycle," and the reason is "because cars and motorcycles are not the same."

2. **Write out the first test for this syllogism.**

   Is there a relationship between "cars" and the fact that "cars are not motorcycles"?

3. **Write out the second test.**

   If cars and motorcycles are not the same thing, is it true that a car must not be a motorcycle?

4. **Write out the third test.**

   If a car is (not + not = is) a motorcycle, would it be true that cars and motorcycles are the same?

5. Is this syllogism true or false?

True, it passes all three tests. As long as the fact "a car is not a motorcycle" is true, then a car shares a relationship with this fact. And it must be the case that if cars and motorcycles are not the same, a car is not a motorcycle.

6. Try to write out a correct syllogism on your own, run the tests to make sure!

I've been using relationships of identity to come up with easy correct syllogisms here. What that means is, think of two things that do or don't share a relationship, then use that in a syllogism. For example, cars are automobiles, red is not green, black is not white, cars and Chevys (Consider a Chevy, it's a car, because all cars are Chevys.)

Chapter 8

1. Write out the third test for syllogism #15.

The third test is if you negate the (2) assertion, the (3) reason should also be negated. So here, if I did not get any money, is it true that I did not give money away? We would say yes, because the seed for getting money is giving money, then if you are not going to get any money it must mean that you did not give any money away.

Consider the following syllogism and answer the questions about it:

Syllogism #16
(1) Consider my real estate investments,
(2) They will get a good return,
(3) Because I created the cause (by planting a mental seed through being generous).

2. **Write out the subject, assertion, and reason.**

The subject is "my real estate investments," the assertion is "[my real estate investments] will get a good return," and the reason is "because I created the cause."

3. **Write out the first test.**

Is there a relationship between "my real estate investments" and creating the cause for getting a good return on them?

4. **Write out the second test.**

Is it true that if I create the cause for a good return I must get a good return?

5. **Write out the third test.**

Is it true that if I did not create the cause for a good return that I will not get a good return?

Consider the following syllogism and answer the questions about it:

Syllogism #17
(1) Consider money,
(2) I'm not going to have enough,
(3) Because I don't give it away.

6. **Write out the subject, assertion, and reason.**

The subject is "money," the assertion is "I'm not going to have enough," and the reason is "because I don't give [money] away."

7. **Write out the first test.**

Is there a relationship between money and giving it away? (Yes, if you give it away you will get it.)

8. **Write out the second test.**

If I do not give away money, must it be the case that I will not have enough?

9. Write out the third test.

If I do give money away, must it be the case that I will have enough?

Chapter 9

1. Write out the first law of seeds.

Seeds are definite, meaning that the content of the result must resemble the content of the cause. For example, being kind will result in my receiving kindness; yelling at someone will result in my being yelled at.

2. Write out the second law of seeds.

Seeds increase; that is, a small act of kindness can bring a large result.

Consider the following syllogism, and then answer the subsequent questions:

<u>Syllogism #18</u>
**(1) Consider giving ten dollars,
(2) The result I get will be much larger (I will get more than ten dollars in the future),
(3) Because mental seeds grow.**

3. Please write out the subject, assertion, and reason.

The subject is "giving ten dollars," the assertion is "result I get will be much larger," and the reason is "because mental seeds grow."

4. Then write out the three tests. Is this syllogism true or false?

According to Tibetan wisdom it would be true. Giving produces a mental seed that will grow, and because mental seeds do grow the result must be larger. Finally, the result would not be larger if it weren't true that mental seeds grow.

Chapter 10

Consider the next syllogism and answer the questions that follow:

Syllogism #21
(1) Consider eating healthy,
(2) It will improve my health,
(3) Because I'm already overweight.

1. Write out the subject, assertion, and reason.

The subject is "eating healthy," the assertion is "eating healthy will improve my health," and the reason is "because I'm overweight already."

2. Run the three tests; is this syllogism true or false?

False. Even if you are overweight, eating healthy may or may not improve your health. If you eat healthy but get in a car accident for example, your health is not likely to improve.

3. If it's false, correct it so that it becomes true.

Just change the reason to be the same as syllogism #20.

Chapter 11

1. Is the reason, "Because not yelling at them won't solve my problems" positive or negative?

Positive; count the negatives, there are two. So this statement is equivalent to saying, "Because yelling at them will solve my problems."

2. What about the reason, "Because it's not possible that the thing doesn't exist." Is it positive or negative?

Positive. Again, two negatives equal a positive. So this statement is equivalent to "Because it must be that the thing exists."

3. **And finally, what about the assertion, "It's definitely not true that just because a thing is empty it doesn't exist." Is it positive or negative?**

Positive again. Don't let the word "empty" throw you off, two negatives is a positive, so this is the same as saying "It's true that a thing that is empty can exist."

Chapter 12

Consider this syllogism and then answer the following questions.

Syllogism #25
(1) Consider my ex-girlfriend/boyfriend,
(2) They're empty,
(3) Because although I/others dislike them, they also have friends.

1. **What is the subject, assertion, and reason?**

The subject is "my ex-girlfriend/boyfriend," the assertion is "they're empty," and the reason is "Because although I/others dislike them, they also have friends."

2. **What is the first test in this case? (Use this example in your answer.)**

   Even though others dislike them, my ex also has friends.

3. **What is the second test? (Use this example in your answer.)**

   If it's true that some like and some dislike my ex, does that mean that they must be empty?

4. **What is the third test? (Use this example in your answer.)**

   If it weren't true that even though some dislike them and others don't, would this mean that they weren't empty?

5. **Is this syllogism true or false?**

   True, although I think you'll have to struggle with the third test a bit. If a person existed that everyone loved—that you had to love (or dislike), because they self-existently had that quality—then that person wouldn't be empty.

Chapter 13

Consider this syllogism and then answer the following questions.

<u>Syllogism #30</u>
(1) Consider the guy/girl of my dreams,
(2) I will meet them,
(3) Because I'm asking my friends to set me up/I spend a lot of time at the bars/I'm beautiful/very generous/easy-going.

1. **What is the first test in this case? (Use this example in your answer.)**

Is there some relationship between the guy/girl of my dreams and asking my friends to set me up/I spend a lot of time at the bars/I'm beautiful/very generous/easy-going?

2. **What is the second test? (Use this example in your answer.)**

Because I'm asking my friends to set me up/I spend a lot of time at the bars/I'm beautiful/very generous/easy-going, must I meet the guy/girl of my dreams?

3. **What is the third test? (Use this example in your answer.)**

If I didn't ask my friends to set me up/spend a lot of time at the bars/wasn't beautiful/very generous/easy-going, would that mean that I could not meet the guy/girl of my dreams?

4. Are these syllogisms true or false? If they're false, write out one that's true (passes the three tests.)

False, of course, because it fails the second and third tests, as all these sorts of arguments will. Sometimes a friend sets you up and it's great, or it might be a disaster. You might meet people at bars, or just get beat up. Lots of beautiful, smart, kind, generous people don't have partners.

So the answer is to plant the seed for what you want: (3) Because I take care of lonely people/help others meet the people they are looking for, and so on.

Chapter 14

Consider this syllogism and then answer the following questions.

Syllogism #32
(1) Consider a pen,
(2) It does not come from a pen factory (the pen factory is not the cause of the pen),
(3) Because my dog sees it as something to chew on.

1. **What is the first test in this case? (Use this example in your answer.)**

   Is there a relationship between the pen and the thing that a dog wants to chew on (yes, they are the same thing).

2. **What is the second test? (Use this example in your answer.)**

   If my dog sees the "pen" as something to chew on, does that mean that a "pen" doesn't come from a pen factory? (Yes, if a pen factory could make a pen that a dog saw as a pen, then pen factories make pens.)

3. **What is the third test? (Use this example in your answer.)**

   If the pen factory is the cause of a pen, would my dog not see it as something to chew on? (Yes, he would see it as something to write with.)

4. **Is this syllogism true or false? Write out your own proof for emptiness using the idea that apparent causes are also empty.**

   Yes, this one is true. If a pen factory was the real cause of the pen then a dog would see it as a pen.

The possible proofs you could come up with are infinite, from simple variations of this one to using what they call in Tibetan logic different functional relationships.

> **For Example**
> For example, a simple variation would be, substitute car for pen and your new reason could be "Because an ant/deer/raccoon sees it as impending doom."

For example:

**Consider my toothbrush,
It doesn't clean my teeth (it's not the real cause),
Because I need to brush them again.**

Think about it: if toothbrushes really cleaned your teeth, would you have to keep brushing them all the time? Why would you need to go to the dentist to get them polished? Or Geshe Michael Roach used this one: your stove doesn't cook your food. If it did, could a gas stove ever have killed anyone? Think about the ant again...

You should struggle with this one a little bit, but if the purpose of a stove is to cook your food, then how can one burn you, or even (if it's gas) explode and kill you? Because the ability of a stove to cook your food isn't coming from the stove, it's coming from you (and so is its ability to burn or kill you).

Chapter 15

1. List the four laws of seeds.

The first law of seeds is that seeds are definite (good causes can only lead to good results, bad causes can only lead to negative results), the second law of seeds is that seeds increase (the result can be much larger than the cause), the third law of seeds is that if you don't do something you can't get the result, and the fourth law of seeds is that if you plant the cause (properly) you must get the result.

 See Appendix B, "The Four Laws of Seeds" for more information.

2. Write out test #3 for the syllogism #34.

If an aspirin does not cure your headache, does that mean that you did not have the seed for it to work?

3. Write out a syllogism for a successful pregnancy. What reason would you give?

Yours could differ slightly, but basically:

Consider my/my partner's pregnancy,
It will be successful,

Because we planted the seed for it by volunteering at a children's hospital and/or by taking care of children.

Chapter 16

1. Which test does the syllogism #35 fail?

Tests #2 and #3. Just because you turn the key doesn't necessarily mean your car will start.

2. Write out test #3 for the syllogism #35.

If I don't turn the key, does that mean it won't start? (Think non-electric starter or popping the clutch—for those of you who have ever driven a stick shift.)

3. Write out test #2 for syllogism #36.

If it's the purpose of my stove to cook my dinner, must it cook my dinner?

4. Write out a correct syllogism for how you will get (create the real cause for) your dinner.

Consider my dinner,
I will get it,
Because I've cooked dinner/provided food for others in the past.

Chapter 17

1. Write out the syllogism for the King of Reasons using your own example.

Again, the possibilities are infinite—just put in a subject you're thinking about.

For example:

Consider getting a raise at work,
It's empty,
Because it depends on something else.

Then, if you want to be more specific:

Consider getting a raise at work,
It's empty,
Because it depends on my seeds—whether or not I've promoted (or tried to recommend) someone else.

2. Write out test #1, #2, and #3 for the syllogism #37, the King of Reasons.

Test #1: Is it true that a thing depends on something else?

Test #2: Just because something depends on something else, does that mean that it has to be empty (not coming from itself)? (Yes, that's almost the definition of emptiness.)

Test #3: If something weren't empty, does that mean it wouldn't depend on something else? (Yes! Now you're starting to get it!)

3. **Write out test #1, #2, and #3 for the syllogism #38.**

   Test #1: Is it true that space also depends on parts? (Yes; up, down, left, right—direction.)

   Test #2: If something depends on parts, does that mean it has to be empty? (Yes, if it depends on something else then it's not coming from itself—it's not self-existent.)

   Test #3: If something were not empty, would it not have to depend on having parts? (Yes, if something were self-existent, it would not have to depend on anything.)

Chapter 18

1. Run the tests on syllogism #41. Does it pass or fail (is it true or false)?

It's true. Can space exist without direction? That is, could something exist in a space without that space having a left and right? Impossible. And if something depends on direction, then it has those parts.

2. Assume your debate partner again answers, "Your reason is not established" after you give them syllogism #42. What would you do next?

You follow the same steps: your (3) reason becomes your new (2) assertion and you give a new reason. For example:

Consider space,
It is so true that there is no thing
that exists that way,
Because you can't tell me one thing that does.

Chapter 19

1. If this was your original syllogism:

<u>Syllogism #15</u>
(1) Consider money,

**(2) I'm going to get some,
(3) Because I give it away.**

And your debate partner answered, "Not necessarily," what does that mean? Use the syllogism in your answer.

"Not necessarily" means that your debate partner thinks that your syllogism failed test #2 and/or #3. So test #2 is, "Just because I give money away doesn't mean that I'm necessarily going to get some." So that means your debate partner thinks your syllogism fails that test ("It's not true that because I give money away I'm going to get some.")

2. **If they answered as above, how would you respond? Give a new syllogism.**

So if they think your syllogism failed test #2, that means that they believe the positive and negative necessity are not true. So you have to prove the positive (or negative) necessity is true.

For example:

It is true that if you give money away you must get some,
Because that's the fourth law of seeds.

3. **Which law is it (of the four laws) that says that if you give something away you must get something in return?**

The fourth law of seeds says that if you plant the seed (create the cause) you must get the result.

Chapter 20

1. **Write down what you want in life; what would make you happy.**

Of course this is going to be different for everyone, but we're looking for success, health, happiness, a nice partner, etc. For example: "I want my project at work to finish successfully."

2. **Write it out as a syllogism; how are you going to make it happen?**

Consider my project at work,
It will finish successfully,
Because I am helping other people
with their projects.

3. **Run the three tests; is your syllogism true? How do you know?**

Test #1: Is there a relationship between your project and helping others with their projects? (Yes, this is one of the seeds for your project to go well.)

Test #2: If you help other people with their projects, must your project finish successfully? (Yes, if you plant the seed correctly and take into account the time gap. The fourth law of seeds says you must get a result.)

Test #3: If I'm not helping other people with their projects, must my project not finish successfully? (Yes, theoretically. Probably, you have helped other people with a project at some point in your life in the past, so you don't have to worry about this. But if you start having trouble finishing projects then you might want to look at this.)

> ⓘ *For more information on this subject, please visit our website at easytibetanlogic.com.*

Appendix B

1. What is the first law of seeds? Give an example of how this could work in your own life.

The first law of seeds is that "seeds are definite," meaning that good must produce good and doing something negative can only produce a bad result. Anything could be an example, as long as it's a true cause and effect relationship. For example, if you give someone else something to eat, it must be the case that you will get something nice to eat in the future. Or a negative example would be if you yell at someone, in the future you must see someone yell back at you.

2. Write out a syllogism that uses the first law of seeds as a reason. (Consider x; y is true, because seeds are definite.)

Again, the examples are infinite, but one example would be:

Consider making money,
It cannot come from cheating others
(cheating others is not the real cause),
Because seeds are definite.

3. What is the second law of seeds? Give an example of what this might look like in your own life.

The second law of seeds is "seeds increase." An example would be the wicked who prosper: someone who is otherwise stingy gives in a small way, then gets a big result years later.

If you think about it, this is a really big problem: if you get a lot of money but you don't know where it really came from, then you don't really know how to keep your prosperity going. You will lose that money sooner or later, or when you do, is it better or worse to have been rich and lost everything or to have never been rich at all?

4. Write out a syllogism that uses the second law of seeds as a reason. (Consider x; y is true, because seeds increase.)

Out of an infinite number of possibilities, here is one:

Consider my new car,
I will get it,
Because I plant small seeds by helping people get where they need to go.

5. What is the third law of seeds? Give an example of how this could work in your own life.

The third law of sees is "Not done, not received": if you don't plant the seed for what you want, you can't get the result.

6. **Write out a syllogism that uses the third law of seeds as a reason. (Consider *x*; *y* is true, because if you don't plant a seed you can't get a result.)**

   One example is:

   Consider violence,
   I will stop seeing it in my world,
   Because I am nonviolent.

7. **What is the fourth law of seeds? Give an example of how this could work in your own life.**

   The final law of seeds is "If you plant the seed, you must get the result." For example, it's not possible that you would give money away and not get something back (eventually, understanding that it takes time for seeds to ripen).

8. **Write out a syllogism that uses the fourth law of seeds as a reason. (Consider *x*, *y* is true, because a seed planted must have a result.)**

   And an example would be:

   Consider my new house,
   I will get it,
   Because I give/help other
   people find a place to stay.

Appendix F: Assumptions

So I mentioned a few times that I would talk about some of the problems people in the know tell me they have with logic. One generally comes from philosophers (those trained in Aristotelian logic), and one from mathematicians. So let's look at the latter first.

Often people in mathematics or mathematics-related fields (finance, for example) are aware of David Hilbert's struggles to prove the foundation of mathematics.

If you're interested in this subject, I highly recommend the highly readable and enjoyable book "Fermat's Last Theorem" by Simon Singh, especially "The Foundations of Knowledge" section of the book, pages 147-164.

He (and others) tried to prove, accepting only a few axioms, that the foundations of mathematics could all be proven through mathematical logic. He failed, principally due to the work of Bertrand Russell and then Kurt Gödel.

Again, if you want more read Mr. Singh's book, but to grossly simplify **Kurt Gödel's work, he proved,** using mathematical logic and Russell's work on subsets, that some things cannot be proven. Essentially, the statement:

> This statement does not have any proof.

Is true.

So let's go back now and talk about the philosophers. The problem of self-referential statements has been known to Western philosophers for millennia—going back to Epimendides, a Cretan, who in the 6th or 7th century BC, proclaimed:

> Cretans, all liars.

You see the problem. If Epimendides is a Cretan, then he must be lying. But if he is lying, then his statement, "All Cretans are liars" must be false—because he's a Cretan, yet he's telling the truth about the fact that all Cretans are liars. Among western philosophers this problem came to be know as "the Liar's Paradox":

This statement is false.

But if the statement is correct about being false, then it's not false—it's true.

It's a problem.

Based on this kind of work, mathematicians and would-be philosophers are always telling me that ultimately, logic isn't valuable—an edifice teetering on the verge of collapse at any moment. Ultimately, they say, if you go looking to prove that a logical system is true—all you'll find is assumptions that can't be proven and a house of cards ready to collapse. That is, if you investigate deeply enough, you will find your mentally created artificial system has no supports: ultimately, it's based on unproven assumptions that can't be proven and therefore ultimately isn't useful.

So I give them an "A" for effort. In principal I like this argument, because Tibetan wisdom says if you leave something alone (in Tibetan, *ma brtags ma dpyad par*) it works fine, but if you keep investigating it you'll find it has no essence—that is to say, it's empty. We agree.

But you can't turn around and use this as an argument for not using logic. Just because something is empty doesn't mean that it doesn't work. If fact, as we've mentioned before, something can only work if it is in fact empty.

There is a famous Tibetan scholar named Khedrup Je who wrote a book on logic called *Dispelling the Darkness of the Mind* (in Tibetan, *yid kyi mun sel*). He gives several powerful reasons for why it's absolutely necessary to study logic. But I started to wonder, after I had studied this book for a while, where were the paradoxes? Western (Aristotelian) logic has tons of them. Where are they in the Tibetan system?

> ⓘ *Some of those reasons given in Khedrup Je's book are targeted more at Buddhists, so I won't get into them all here. But it does have a clue how to solve our problem, which I'll mention later.*

We talked in chapter two about the possible connection between Aristotelian and Tibetan logic; there are a lot of similarities. But then again, there are differences. Why?

So I thought, "I wonder what the liar's paradox would look like in a Tibetan syllogism." So let's take a look; maybe it would look something like:

(1) Consider the statement, "All Cretans are liars,"
(2) It's both true and false,
(3) Because that statement is self-contradictory.

So remember, Gödel's proof says that the fact that this statement can't be determined to be true or false is a big problem. But what's the problem? Here I have written a perfectly good syllogism that expresses a truth statement about the "problem question." What does it prove? Really, it only proves that, with human language, you can make self-contradictory statements. So what? How does that discredit logic as a system? In other words, what does the fact that the grammatical rules of English allow you to make a self-contradictory statement prove? Only that the grammatical rules of English aren't a logical system that you can rely on.

So let's write the liar's "paradox" out again, this time trying to prove something that is not true using the Tibetan wisdom tradition's rules for logical thought (rather than English grammar). Wouldn't that be what was actually necessary to invalidate logic as a system? That you could use it to prove something false was true, or that something true was false? So, if I write it out that way, it might look like:

(1) Consider Epimendides' statement, "All Cretans are liars,"
(2) It's true,
(3) Because all Cretans are liars.

True or false? False. Why? Because all Cretans are not liars. Why? Because we have already at least one example of a Cretan telling the truth (our friend Epimendides). Or if you want to stick to the idea that we can't determine the truth or falsity of Epimendides' statement (is it neither true nor false or both true and false?), then all I need is one example of a Cretan telling the truth to disprove this syllogism. (I'm sure one said something true somewhere, if not Epimendides himself.)

So you see, using the Tibetan wisdom tradition's rules for logical thought, there is no paradox that can be stated as a syllogism. Any way you try to state the "paradox" will require you to give a reason that will turn out to be false. So there's no paradox there.

So what about the more pure form of the argument; that is, the western philosophical form of the Liar's Paradox? Let's see what that one might look like:

(1) Consider the statement, "This statement is false,"
(2) It's false,
(3) Because the statement itself says it is false.

Then we can answer, "Not necessarily." Just because a statement makes a claim to be false doesn't mean that it must necessarily be false. Take, for example, the statement, 'This statement is false.'" Again, if you want to maintain that this statement can't be said to be false.

But anyway, if I haven't given you a headache by now, let's move on and discuss, on a more theoretical level, why all those mathematicians failed to find a logical foundation for mathematics.

As we said before, Tibetan wisdom says that if you leave something alone—that is, you don't put too much effort into analyzing it—it will work pretty much as you expect. But if you take the time to analyze something, what you'll see is that you're making a lot of assumptions that will turn out to be false, because, in the end, all things are empty (but more on that in the next appendix).

In Tibetan logic there are two ways of knowing something exists (again, to prove something exists is to prove that it is true):

1. Direct valid perception
2. Indirect valid perception

Direct valid perception is easy to understand; this just means what you can perceive directly with your senses. For example, how do you know if something is blue? You see it with eyes. Is something hot or cold? You touch it. Indirect valid perception is deductive logic. In other words, everything we studied in this book (I'm not going to review it all here).

But the interesting thing is, from a Tibetan logic point of view, that indirect valid perception is dependent on direct valid perception. Khedrup Je, who we quoted before, says this in his book *"Dispelling the Darkness of the Mind"*:

> And establishing that kind of reasoning as flawless depends on using the three tests, and all three tests in turn eventually have to be established through direct correct perception. If it was the case that you could establish something as true using only indirect perception, then you have the problem of infinite regression.

So, in the case of mathematics, if it's true that ultimately the way to know something is to prove that it exists, how do you prove that numbers exist? You have to count something.

This is from Bertrand Russell:

> 'But,' you might say, 'none of this shakes my belief that 2 and 2 are 4.' You are quite right, except in marginal cases—and it is only in marginal cases that you are doubtful whether a certain animal is a dog or a certain length is less than a metre. Two must be of something, and the proposition '2 and 2 are 4' is useless unless it can be applied. Two dogs and two dogs are certainly four dogs, but cases arise in which you are doubtful as to whether two of them are

dogs. 'Well, at any rate, there are four animals,' you might say. But there are microorganisms concerning which it is doubtful whether they are animals or plants. 'Well, then living organisms,' you say. But there are things of which it is doubtful whether they are living or not. You will be driven into say: 'Two entities and two entities are four entities.' When you have told me what you mean by 'entity', we will resume the argument.

So the reason why mathematicians can't solve their issues with the foundation of mathematics is because they're trying to keep it abstract: if you want to prove the mathematics logically you eventually have to relate it to something you can verify with a direct perception: something you can confirm directly with your senses. If you keep what you're doing abstract then you ultimately won't be able to confirm it. Which is what Bertrand Russell found.

So Bertrand Russell's doubts don't really seem to be a problem to me. Why? Yes, you can count something. When you go to count something, can you be sure of what you are counting? Yes, if it fits the definition for that thing. Something is a dog if it fits your definition for what a dog is. What if it doesn't fit that definition for someone else? Why would you expect it to? When you analyze the dog to find why it is a dog, you will find nothing, because the thing you take for a dog, coming from its own side, is actually only coming from you. We already know that a pen for one person is a chew toy for a dog. But that the dog sees it as a chew toy in no way invalidates that it's a pen for me. If a thing is different from one person to the next, that's just because they have different seeds. That doesn't mean you can't count them; they're all pens for me.

So let's try a syllogism:

(1) Consider mathematics,
(2) You can prove out its axioms,
(3) Because we can make, in all cases, true and false value judgments.

If you say, "Your reason is not established," I would reply:

(1) Consider mathematics,
(2) We can make, in all cases, true or false value judgments,
(3) Because all Tibetan logic syllogisms are either true or false.

I haven't studied mathematic logic in depth, so to be honest, I'm not sure if that last one is true or false myself; I might answer to that one, "Your reason is not established," because I don't know if there's a direct relationship between mathematics and Tibetan logic or not (if the Tibetan logic system of proof can be applied to mathematics).

But let's get back to where I started this appendix:

> **(1) Consider logic,**
> **(2) It is supremely useful in your life,**
> **(3) Because in all cases it will help you make true or false value judgments about what is happening to you in your life.**

This one I'm pretty sure about; you test it out.

Appendix G:
Even Emptiness must be Empty

The last thing I thought I'd write about in this book (other than where you can go next for more information) is the emptiness of emptiness. There's one last complaint I sometimes get from philosophers who equate the teaching on emptiness to relativism: Is everything relative?

When we say that everything is coming from you (well, more correctly, your seeds,) that sounds like we're saying, "Everything is relative." To which there is an easy disproof: if everything is relative, then so is that statement itself—that is, if everything is relative then that statement itself is also relative, which means that everything cannot be relative. It's self-contradictory, like our liar's paradox from the last appendix.

So… we're not saying that. Saying everything is empty is not the same as saying everything is relative, because in Tibetan wisdom one thing is not relative: emptiness. In the Tibetan wisdom tradition, if you want to divide every existing thing into two sets, one way is to divide them into the set of ultimate and the set of relative things. Everything you see is relative, but not all things are relative. What things are not relative? Emptiness.

How is emptiness not relative? It is true of all things: show me something that exists, and I will show you something that is empty.

So how do we avoid self-contradiction? Relativity itself cannot be relative. But emptiness can be empty. That's the difference.

So how is emptiness empty? If we use the definition of emptiness we gave before (review chapter ten, "Negation") then emptiness is also nothing other than a perception on parts, forced on us by our seeds. Everything we perceive is forced on us by our seeds, nothing is other than that. Not even that fact itself.

As a syllogism (using the King of Reasons from chapter sixteen):

(1) Consider emptiness,
(2) It is also empty,
(3) Because it is dependently originated.

So to quote Darth Vader, "There is no conflict."

Appendix H: Additional Resources

So if you want to learn more you have several options. Like I've said, the best option is to practice! But if you want to read or study this subject more, there are a few written and online materials you can use.

I've started a website at www.easytibetanlogic.com where I'll occasionally add materials and links.

If you don't mind studying some Buddhist materials, you can download free materials from the Asian Classics Institute (ACI), which offers a course on Buddhist logic: "ACI course 13: The Art of Reasoning, Level 2 of Buddhist Logic and Perception (Pramana)." You can download it for free at:

http://acidharma.org/aci/online/onlinefr.html

There are also some books you can get; my favorite is "Pointing the Way to Reasoning" by Sera Mey Khensur Rinpoche Geshe Lobsang Tharchin (available from the Mahayana Sutra and Tantra Press). And also, from the same author, "The Logic and Debate Tradition of India, Tibet, and Mongolia." (But I warn you, that book is not for the faint of heart.)

But again, the best thing you can do is practice. Find a partner and help them learn:

    (1) Consider logic,
    (2) I will be good at it,
    (3) Because I'll plant seeds by teaching it to others.

Enjoy and good luck.

The Author

Vice President of Creative Media for the Diamond Cutter Institute, Eric Brinkman has always been interested in logic and philosophy, but began studying Tibetan Buddhism in July 2000. Since then has traveled to Tibetan monasteries in India and studied around the US with both Tibetan and American teachers. He has lectured on and taught logic all over the world, including Japan, Singapore, England, and Russia, and is currently coaching and working on a documentary film.

Fore more information visit his website at
www.ericmichaelbrinkman.com.

A SPIRITUAL RENEGADE'S guide to the GOOD LIFE

"Lama Marut is a great teacher, a master...
He's changed me in just about every way.
I'm happy, and I know how to perpetuate that."
—**Lindsay Crouse**, Academy Award–nominated actress

LAMA MARUT

www.ingramcontent.com/pod-product-compliance
Lightning Source LLC
Chambersburg PA
CBHW020931090426
42736CB00010B/1102